Family Walks
in
Surrey

Norman Bonney

HIGH INTEREST · LOW MILEAGE

Scarthin Books of Cromford
Derbyshire
1994

Family Walks Series

The Country Code

Guard against all risk of fire
Fasten all gates
Keep your dogs under proper control
Keep to public paths across farmland
Avoid damaging fences, hedges and walls
Leave no litter
Safeguard water supplies
Make no unnecessary noise
Protect wildlife, plants and trees
Go carefully along country roads
Respect the life of the countryside

Published 1994

Phototypesetting by Paragon Typesetters, Queensferry, Clwyd

Printed by Redwood Books

ISBN 0 907758 74 6

Cover illustration by Andrew Ravenwood

The sandy shores of Frensham Little Pond (walk 2)

Preface

Although there are many rambling clubs in London and the Home Counties, some families are not yet ready to join these but would like to go walking. It is hoped that these walks will be a gentle introduction to the delights that abound in this lovely county. Although primarily designed for adults with children they are suitable for anybody. In some instances the more energetic could even combine two of these walks. For example the North Downs Way could connect St Martha's with the Newlands Corner walk. The great beauty and diversity of Surrey can only be fully appreciated if you get off the main highway and away from the crowded well-known beauty spots into the depth of the surprisingly unspoilt countryside. Youngsters with their famillies can there enjoy a freedom denied in the busy towns.

Acknowledgements

I would like to thank my wife Nancy for accompanying me on these walks and for typing most of the book. Thanks are also due to my daughter Rosemary, son-in-law Shawn and son Martin who came out on some of the walks and made their contribution to the typing.

About the author

A Londoner by birth, Norman Bonney is a retired government administrator who spent some of his life in Southport and Southend on Sea. Most of the time, however, he has lived in Surrey. In early days he was a member of a local Youth Hostel group so that then and later he led many walks for clubs. Since retirement he has taken up watercolour painting but his main interest continues to be walking both in this country and abroad. His wife, a schoolteacher, keeps him up to date with her experiences of school journeys. Though no longer living in Surrey his son and daughter continue to be keen walkers. His grandson is too young to walk but already loves going on rambles from the view he obtains from the carrier on his parents' backs.

Contents

Map of the area

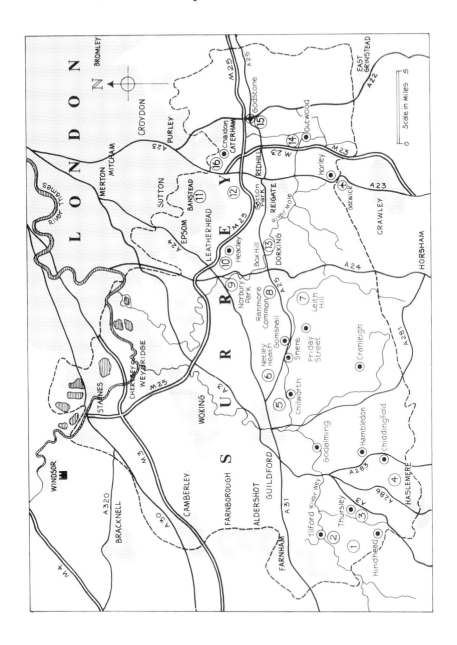

Introduction

The focus of this book like others in the series is upon 'Family Walks.' From the experience of our own family and from school journeys, many children like to walk five or six miles. Some are even keen to do an extra walk in the evening. For those who at first may find such a distance daunting, there are cut off points on many routes to enable you to do a shorter walk or amble. This may allow you longer time for play. On the walks there are a variety of things to interest youngsters. Once rambling has got into the blood it often lasts a lifetime. At the age of seven my son had done the Gable traverse, a high level walk in the Lakes and on another holiday at the age of 14 he had walked the whole of the Offa's Dyke long distance path. This was followed up with many other long distance paths.

Some of the walks in this book touch on two long distance paths: the North Downs Way (marked with an acorn sign) which runs from Farnham to Dover (141 miles) and the more recently developed Greensand Way from Haslemere to Ham Street in Kent (105 miles).

We are very lucky in having in the small county of Surrey such a variety of scenery. Despite the urban sprawl from London, the Green Belt has helped to protect some land. There are more trees per acre than in any other county of England. Most are deciduous woods covered with bluebells in springtime. Surrey's winding lanes, gentle hills, village greens and its commons still make it one of the most beautiful areas to visit.

In a simplified form the main geological features of the county can be divided into five areas. In the north-west corner are the Bagshot Downs. Beneath that and spreading eastwards right up to the Thames are the London Clays. South of that are the chalk North Downs: starting as the Hogs Back, a narrow strip between Farnham and Guildford, this widens out and continues on to Kent. Nearly half of our walks are around this chalk down (Routes 6, 8 to 12 and 16). Where there are horses this can sometimes be muddy, particularly if the chalk is capped by clay or loam, but usually you can find a way round the mud. Near the southern escarpment you may come across the unmarked pill boxes set up as a line of defence during the Second World War. Many were built by the Canadian Army who were stationed in the area.

Beneath the downs are the Lower Greensand Hills, the fourth geological area, that in the south-west go right down as the broad end of a triangle to the county border. The sand beds have this name because in some of them are small grains of the greenish mineral glauconite, hydrated silicate of iron and potassium. This chemical is used in the manufacture of green paint and for water softening. In this area the acidity of the ground leads to extensive heathland.

Heaths are in decline throughout Europe and in recent years the county authorities have been making terrific efforts to protect what remains (Routes 1 to 3). The whole area is rich in wildlife and it can be fun to make a list of what you find on both the land and water. But take care not to disturb the wild creatures and the vegetation. Further east the Greensand Hills are capped by churt which has prevented erosion as you can investigate on the walk to our highest hill (Leith Hill on Route 7). Moving

7

further over to the east again we reach a narrow strip of two types of Upper Greensand, one of which is called malmstone and at one time was quarried around Godstone.

Away from the chalk all the remaining walks are on or close to the sandy areas except for one which is on the Weald. This broad band of clay for many centuries cut London off from Sussex during the wet winter months. Route 14 has been selected to show on part of this walk what this wooded area would have been like before the land was drained and cleared of some of the trees. There are many footpaths in the Weald and elsewhere but these will have to be left for another occasion.

It is hard to imagine that before the industrial revolution there was so much industry in Surrey. Thanks to ample timber for charcoal burning, the glass industry flourished in Chiddingfold and then spread over the Sussex border and on to Ewhurst and Alfold. Later there was such a clamour about the destruction of wood that in 1615, its use was prohibited and the industry went to London where coal could be used.

Charcoal was also used for the iron industry. Streams were dammed up to form hammer ponds where the fall of water was used to work a pair of bellows for the blast furnace and to raise and let fall a hammer. On the Tillingbourne there were also gunpowder, brass and wire works and many water mills for corn and cloth milling.

Industry changed the scenery of this sandy area south of the A25. The timber stocks were denuded, altering the appearance of the landscape, in some places permanently. At Blackheath south of St Martha's (Route 5) for example, it was not until the scots pine had seeded that the heathland again started to cover the light porous soils.

Allowing sufficient time

An average adult walker does about 2½ miles per hour. You are a better judge of what your children can do. Some children can keep up with that whilst some little ones may only go about a mile an hour. It is better to over-estimate rather than under-estimate the time required, to allow time for play and not to rush the last part of the route. For little ones it could be useful to have a carrier frame in reserve so that you can carry them on your back.

What to wear

Good comfortable trainers, particularly the boot variety are quite adequate for Surrey. However, if you are really enthusastic walkers, it is worth investing in walking boots for all the family. Cagoules are a must and waterproof trousers a useful extra if you are going to do much winter walking. Cords are better than jeans, but modern leggings are fine if you have over-trousers. It is worth having a woolly hat, and several thin jumpers are better than one thick one. Don't forget a small rucksack for carrying picnics, drinks and cameras and a plastic map case to keep your book dry.

Route finding

The maps in this book, taken in conjunction with the directions provided should be sufficient to find your way. For those who like to carry Ordnance Survey maps when out walking, Landranger sheets 186 and 187, and in the larger scale Pathfinder series, sheets 1206, 1207, 1225, 1226, 1227 and 1245, cover all the walks.

Refreshments

I have tried to indicate suitable places for refreshment. It may be only a kiosk but most are well-supplied and on a hot day are welcome for a drink or ice-cream. The landlords of the pubs en route normally allow children accompanied by adults on to their premises but bear in mind some hostelries may have changed hands. In any event it is better to show your children are well behaved and negotiate your position. Many of you would prefer a picnic on some sunny hillside.

Conclusion

On some of the walks you are told a little about the flora and fauna to look out for. If you are quiet you may come across wildlife anywhere. I have surprised deer and foxes in very unusual places.

Please remember not to pick the flowers. Primroses had almost disappeared with people digging up plants and the use of weed killers. However, if these and other scarce plants are allowed to seed they soon spread again.

Remember the rest of the country code. Ramblers need to keep landowners and farmers on their side. Urge your offspring to take a responsible attitude towards the countryside and in particular take your litter home.

Finally I hope you have as much fun trying out these walks as I had in devising the routes.

Bridge over the River Wey at Tilford (walk 2)

9

Map Key

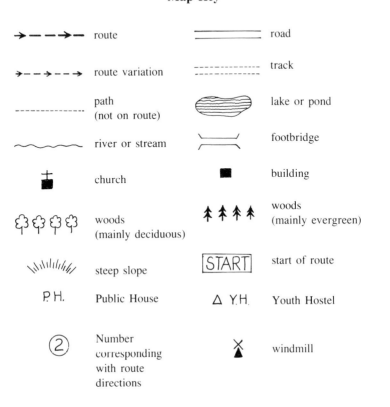

➤– –➤–	route	══════	road
➤– –➤– –➤	route variation	- - - - - - -	track
- - - - - -	path (not on route)	🌊	lake or pond
∿∿∿	river or stream	⌣⌣	footbridge
☩	church	■	building
🌳🌳🌳🌳	woods (mainly deciduous)	🌲🌲🌲🌲	woods (mainly evergreen)
\\\⎮⎮⎮///	steep slope	START	start of route
P. H.	Public House	△ Y.H.	Youth Hostel
②	Number corresponding with route directions	✕	windmill

Route 1

Frensham Great Pond and the Devil's Jumps

Outline
Frensham Common − Churt Common − The Devil's Jumps −
Pride of the Valley − Frensham Common.

Summary
This ramble is close to the south-west corner of Surrey and is over dry sandy heathlands suitable for walks at any time of year.

Attractions
The walk starts from the large car park at Frensham Great Pond. Beyond the toilet and refreshment hut there is a sandy beach and a section of the lake reserved for children, ideal for sunbathing and paddling. Dogs are prohibited from this play area to ensure it remains clean. There is ample room to exercise pets elsewhere.

The Great Pond and its neighbour the Little Pond (see Route 2) were created in the 13th century by monks to supply fish for the Bishop of Winchester. The lakes were drained in the Second World War to prevent them being a landmark for incoming bombers but they have been restocked and are now fished by local clubs. (If you have time the remains of Waverley Abbey, a Cistercian Monastery founded in 1128 and a few miles north-west of these two walks is well worth a visit.) At any time of year the water and common land is rich in bird life and on a warm day you may be lucky and spy some sand lizards basking in the sun. To the east on the crest of the common are a line of four Bronze Age bowl barrows. The southernmost barrow shows signs of past excavation but no record of these activities was kept.

The monument on the open hillside is to commemorate the bequest of the common to the National Trust by W.A. Robertson whose two brothes died in the First World War.

At the southern end of the walk you can climb one of the Devil's Jumps. Legend has it that the devil amused himself by jumping from one to another until Thor threw a block of sandstone at him. Whether or not you believe the old tale that this Norse god still haunts the neighbourhood, the block remains and is a good viewpoint for the surrounding countryside.

In Rushmoor there is Anna's Country Store where children may be interested in a good selection of rabbits, guinea pigs, birds and fish.

Refreshments
There is a refreshment hut between the car park and the lake, which is open from Easter to September and if the weather is kind at weekends into October. South of the Devil's Jumps the hotel Pride of the Valley has a children's play area.

Route 1

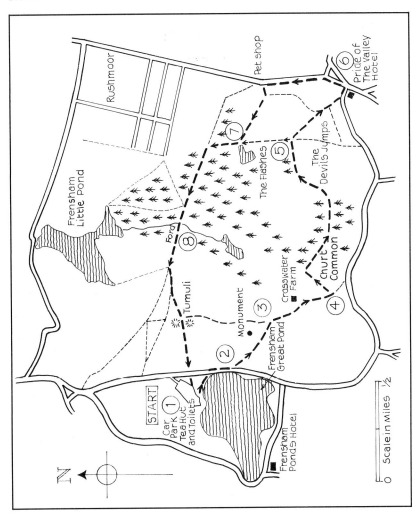

Route 1

Frensham Great Pond and the Devil's Jumps   5 miles
(Variations 4 miles and 1¾ miles)

Start

From the car park on the minor road to the Frensham Hotel off the A287 Farnham—Hindhead road (GR 845405). (The car park shown off the A287 on some OS maps no longer exists. This is being restored to heathland to enhance both the landscape and wildlife value of the site.)

Route

1. *On the pond side of the tea hut skirt the pond along the metal barrier. Take the right-hand turning nearest the lake by the conservation area.*

2. *When the lake and road become close bear off to the left under a smallish oak tree. Take care crossing the A287. Follow the path marked 'no horses' and then under another oak tree, before going uphill, passing a monument on the left.*

3. *At the crossroads of paths at the top of the hill turn right. (If doing the shortest walk you can look back to obtain a good view of the lake and then turn left along the ridge joining the main walk again by the tumuli at 9.) Fifty yards on at another junction of paths keep straight on and drop down the slope. At the bottom, six paths meet. Take the bridleway with the field on the left where there may be some pigs. Further on at the Crosswater Farm entrance this bridleway changes to a metalled road.*

4. *Follow this road until you reach a permitted bridle track on the left marked 'Tanglewood', by the side of Churt Common. Turn left on this and at the other end of the fenced track turn right. This bridleway has some twists in it but can easily be followed continuing eastwards for about ¾ mile. This starts in the woods then there is some open heathland to the left and then some woods again before meeting a junction of paths including a bridleway going from north to south.*

5. *At this junction you will need to cross the bridleway and then take the second path which goes diagonally off to the right of the original path and after a short distance the path climbs a long flight of steps. After having a good look round from the rocks you should descend the hill continuing roughly in the same southerly direction as before. As a landmark you will spot some glasshouses beyond where you are going. Those who do not have the energy can take the bridleway, first turning right at the junction and about ⅓ mile ahead turn left. About ¼ mile on you will meet the energetic ones coming down the hill and turn right to join them. After following this path between boundary fences you will come out on the road. Turn left and a short distance ahead you will come to the Pride of the Valley hotel at a junction.*

13

6. From the hotel go north following the road signposted to *Rushmoor* and *Tilford*. Take care walking on this road. At slightly less than ½ mile turn left at the footpath sign. (If you wish to visit the pet shop by the garage you will need to go a little further up the road and return.) One hundred yards ahead on reaching a bridleway turn right.

7. About ¼ mile ahead, on reaching another path, turn right. The map shows the Flashes just beyond this junction, an area of shallow water which in dry weather disappears. On reaching the metalled road, turn left.

8. After crossing a ford walk on until you see three houses on the left. Just beyond this on the left you will see a grassy path going up the hillside. Follow this, ignoring the sharp left-hand turn about 20 yards ahead.

9. Follow the path up the ridge where there is a group of tumuli. The path just beyond may sometimes be blocked for conservation reasons. If so turn right along the ridge but shortly take the alternative path down the hill back to Frensham. Cross the main road with care and follow the path straight on between fences back to the tea hut and starting point.

Shorter variations
1¾ miles:
See 3 above for the shortest walk.
4 miles:
As for 1 to 4 above, then − if you wish to reduce the length of the walk instead of turning right for the Devil's Jumps at 5 turn left on a bridleway and rejoin the walk at 7 but continue straight on to reach the road detailed.

Public Transport
There is a regular bus service from Aldershot via Farnham which goes close to the car park before going onto the Frensham Hotel, Hindhead and Haslemere.

Steps near Frensham Little Pond

14

Tilford and Frensham Little Pond

Outline
Tilford — Frensham Little Pond — Pierrepont Home Farm — Tilford Mill Bridge — Tilford.

Summary
Start this walk from delightful Tilford village green or, if you prefer, do a figure-of-eight walk by starting from the Frensham Little Pond car park. From this last spot you could also do a short stroll just round the lake. This stretch of water always has something of interest.

Attractions
The north and south branch of the River Wey meet in the village of Tilford. The car park overlooks the river and an ancient bridge. Opposite is the village green where cricket is played most summer weekends.

After passing the Barley Mow you reach the famous 800 year old Tilford Oak at the end of the green. William Cobbett called this the finest tree he had ever seen. In 1952 it had a girth of 26½ ft at 5 ft high. It is still standing but by now it is in decline and you will find some of its trunk has to be protected by corrugated iron.

The walk continues through woodland close to the southern branch of the River Wey to Frensham Little Pond. The walk circuiting the lake could be cut out but you must visit the sandy shore of the pond for there are usually swans, ducks and geese on the water. See Route 1 for more details of the area. Waverley Abbey is only a few miles north-west of Tilford. On the return the walk crosses the river and passes Pierrepont Farm where you may be lucky to see a herd of Jersey cows, then goes through a dark pine wood before coming out at a group of stables. After another stretch of woodland cross over the northern branch of the River Wey before returning to the village.

Refreshments
The Barley Mow does not have a license to permit children into the pub but it does have a tea house which opens when there is sufficient trade. See also Route 1 for other suggestions.

Public Transport
The restricted service is of no use to ramblers.

Route 2

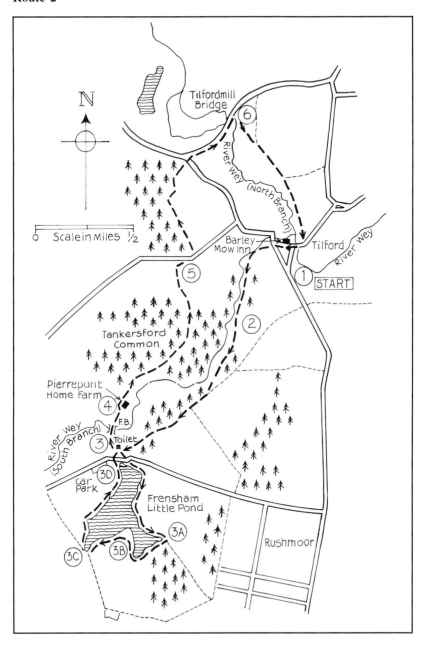

16

Route 2

Tilford and Frensham Little Pond

7¼ miles
(Variations 4½ and 2¾ miles)

Start

You can start this walk from Tilford village green (GR 873434). Alternatively you could do the shorter walks by starting from Frensham Little Pond car park (GR 858418).

Route

1. *From Tilford car park bordering the River Wey and facing the cricket green, go past the Barley Mow pub and the Tilford Oak. Opposite the oak at the western end of the green (before reaching the river bridge) take the shingle track and turn right through an avenue of cupressus in a nursery growing many varieties of cupressus. Go through a gate at the end and continue through a wood with glimpses of the Southern Branch of the River Wey.*

2. *On reaching a track, turn right. Stay on this, ignoring another track that leads down to a house. In the autumn look out for fungi including shaggy ink caps. Go through a stile and turn right. Ignore a path going off to the left 200 yards ahead and continue to a junction of paths by the toilets.*

3. *From the Tilford path turn left by the toilets and the pond should be in view. Cross the metalled road and take the path to the left of the pond and after about 25 yards turn right to approach the pond. The main path skirts a small beach. Keep on this path and shortly a field can be seen on the left-hand side which is used for growing seedling conifers. At a Y-junction of paths take either, for they join again after a short time.*

3a. *At NT sign take a path off to the right through a fence. Then branch right again over a little wooden bridge and a railway sleeper walkway over some wetlands. Once through the woods turn right.*

3b. *When the pond is in view again, turn left and on reaching a heather hillside turn right by a bridleway.*

3c. *25 yards further on at a junction of paths turn right again to follow the path round the pond. To do this you will need to turn right again on reaching some heathland. The sandy beach would be a good spot for children to play and watch the birds on the water.*

3d. *On reaching the car park, cross over and take the track opposite to the right. This leads back to the toilets.*

4. On the ladies' side of the toilets take bridleway 513. After about 50 yards turn right downhill past a keepers cottage and cross a footbridge (the ford across the River Wey could be too deep).

5. At Pierrepont Farm you may be lucky and see some Jersey cows. Turn right here on a bridleway and keep straight on where a farm track turns off to the right. After going through a dark pine wood the path bears right between two lots of riding stables.

6. When the track meets a metalled road cross straight over and follow the bridleway up to another road. Cross this and take Sheephatch Lane opposite.

7. Cross Tilford Mill Bridge over the northern branch of the River Wey and almost immediately turn right on a footpath. Keep straight on ignoring a path to the right but after passing a large house with interesting trimmed trees take the right-hand bridleway. At the end of this turn right and the car park can be seen across the bridge.

Variations
Start at Frensham Little Pond car park. *4½ miles* Follow the directions from 4 onwards. *2¾ miles* Turn eastwards past the end of the pond and take the first path to the right. This is where the path from the toilets joins and you can circuit the pond (sometimes out of sight) as detailed in 3 to 3d above.

The Barley Mow, Tilford

18

Route 3   6 miles
(Variation 3 miles)

Thursley and Highcombe Bottom

Outline

West of Thursley − Smallbrook − Hedge Farm − Little Cowdrey Farm − Highcombe Bottom − Thursley.

Summary

This walk explores the quieter end of Hindhead, one of Surrey's best-known beauty spots. It was notorious for three criminals who were hung on the highest spot, Gibbet Hill, in 1787 for murdering a sailor.

Attractions

Many motorists driving from Hindhead to Guildford on the Portsmouth Road have circled and looked down on the Devil's Punch Bowl. On this walk we approach this National Trust area from the north, a much quieter way. Many of the paths are dry and sandy with woods and bracken to play hide and seek. The walk first goes through picturesque farmland and then climbs up part of the Greensand Way before going down to Highcombe Bottom and the remote Hindhead Youth Hostel. After crossing the stream, gradually climb up the valley and woods to the starting point. You can make a much shorter walk by cutting across the valley at Ridgeway Farm.

Start this walk just to the west of Thursley. If you have time, besides visiting the pub (see below) it is worth looking around the village. It has no centre but there are many interesting old cottages dating back to the 16th and 18th centuries. There is also a church further south. It would have been better if the Victorians had not done their restoration work but two windows and some walling of the original Saxon building remain.

Refreshments

Children are welcome at the Three Horseshoes, a charming country pub in Thursley.

Public Transport

The very restricted bus service is of no use for ramblers.

Route 3

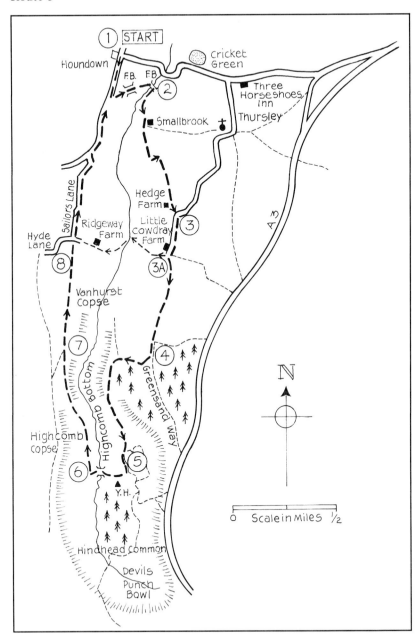

Route 3

Thursley and Highcombe Bottom

6 miles
(Variation 3 miles)

Start

If approaching from the A3, turn off the dual carriageway at the Thursley sign. After going through the village and round a sharp bend you will reach a T-junction. Go straight across this on to a dirt track and park at a suitable spot (GR 893399).

Route

1. *From the car parking area return to the road and walk southwards along it. After passing a minor road on the right look out for a path to the left by a double bend sign. Follow this path downhill and a hundred yards further on you will cross a small footbridge. After crossing another stile the descent continues to another footbridge.*

2. *Walk over the bridge and cross the next stile and turn right on to a narrow metalled road. At Smallbrook House keep straight on along the Greensand Way (GW waymarked). Keep uphill still along the metalled road but continue on the path when the road turns to Haybrook Barn. At the top of the hill bear left over stile at GW sign. Go straight uphill and across the next stile. Look out for the rabbits. There are lots of holes round here. Continue round the left-hand side of Hedge Farm coming out on a metalled road.*

3. *Turn right on this road. Follow the GW signs and close to Little Cowdrey Farm the main walk bears slightly left off the metalled road at signpost. This track leads to Punchbowl Farm (ignore the path up the steps but follow the red arrow).*

4. *At the NT sign take the right-hand fork. Keep straight on to the Y-junction. All this time you will see a field over to your right. Close to where this ends take the right-hand fork and at the next junction bear right. Lots of puffballs can be seen here in the autumn. Despite all the right turns the path is still actually bearing to the left. As we come over the brow of the hill the path descends to the left and comes out on to open moorland. Keep to the main track. Ignore the track on the left at the corner of the fence.*

5. *Further on there is a NT warden's cottage on the left (Gnome Cottage) and at a T-junction by a YHA sign turn right. After passing the Youth Hostel at a turning circle turn right on nature trail number 7 to Highcombe Bottom. The path turns steeply downhill. Bear right at the Y-junction. The path twists down to a stream and a little bridge. Turn left uphill. This path is fun, going through a bed of flints in a sort of gorge.*

6. *Turn right at the unnumbered nature trail sign. You come to Highcombe Copse. Ignore the permissive bridleway to the very pretty cottage on the right.*

7. *Turn right at the crossroads of paths on the ridge. There are Scots pines on the left. You will see lots of fungi in the autumn.*

8. *Follow on to emerge on Sailor's Lane and continue straight down. When this lane joins Thursley Road turn right and follow this back to where you left your car.*

Variation
    follow 1 to 3 above, then:
3a.*Keep on the metalled road bearing round to the right. This soon becomes a bridleway and just beyond Ridgeway Farm turn right on Sailor's Lane to join the main walk again at 8.*

Hindhead Youth Hostel, hidden deep in the Devil's Punchbowl

22

Chiddingfold and Hambledon

Outline
Chiddingfold – Witley Station – Hambledon – Chiddingfold.

Summary
This is our most southerly walk in Surrey through beautiful undulating countryside. Much of the walk is on dry sandy paths going through woodland and arable farmland.

Attractions
Glass-making was an important industry in Chiddingfold from 1300 until suppressed by Elizabeth I following complaints about the French- and German-owned furnaces. Some of the glass was used in St Stephen's Chapel, now part of the House of Commons, and St George's Chapel, Windsor. Some fragments of glass collected from the old glassworks sites have been used to make the back window of the parish church. The church dates from 1190 but was heavily restored in Victorian times.

Opposite are some Georgian houses and the timber-framed Crown inn which was built for Cistercian monks. The inn has the oldest licence in Surrey.

After leaving Chiddingfold we make our way through woodland and over a stream to Witley Station. The walk does not cross the railway line, but if you want to visit the Lockwood Donkey Sanctuary you will need to do this. It is about ½ mile ahead. The sanctuary for ageing donkeys also has poultry and a few goats, horses, rabbits, cats and dogs (GR 938398).

From the station we walk on to the Merry Harriers Inn and beautiful Hambledon Church with a wooden steeple. In the churchyard there is the usual old yew but this one has a hollow trunk which some claim can accommodate as many as 12 people. This is the furthest we go to the north-east, but before turning it is worth going on by the path next to the walled churchyard. Opposite the wall is the entrance to a disused lime kiln with a notice that it was in use until the 19th century.

From the church we drop downhill to the southern end of Hambledon and then follow a dry bridlepath. On the right, small ponds can be seen through the woods. We then follow the main road for a short way passing the Winterton Arms before following another path back to Chiddingford.

Refreshments
There are numerous pubs and inns on this walk. In the village is the Crown famous for its sausages, the Swan and also Roberts Stores. Just north of the village is the Winterton Arms and by Witley Station there is the Pig 'n' Whistle. At Hambledon for fun the 16th century Merry Harriers advertises warm beer and lousy food but welcomes hikers and has a swing in the garden.

Route 4

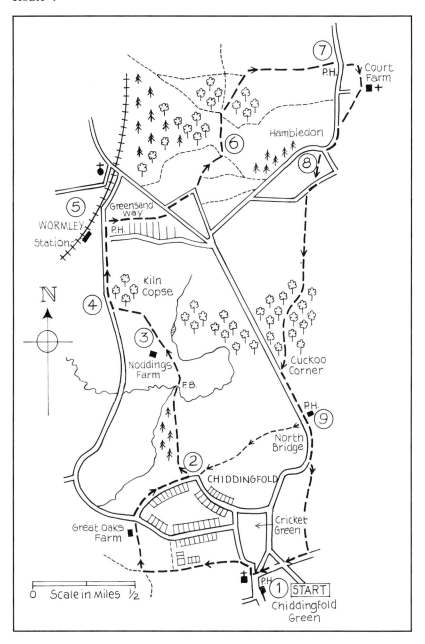

Route 4

Chiddingfold and Hambledon

7 miles
(Variation 5 miles)

Start

Chiddingfold is on the A283 from Milford to Arundel. You can park on the quiet side of the green just to the east of the main road (GR 962355). If you are doing the shorter walk you will need to park at either Witley Station (see 5 below GR 948379) or the Winterton Arms (GR 965365) which are further north and are respectively west and east of the main road.

Route

1. *Cross the main road by the village pond north of the parish church and after crossing the minor road turn right for about 50 yards before going left by the public footpath sign. Pass a cemetery on the left, go through a kissing gate, then another at the end of the path before joining a quiet road. Continue straight on along a footpath when the road bears to the right. Cross two stiles keeping to the right-hand upper path. About a third of the way across the field (150 yards) take a footpath to the right going over two stiles close together. There are double stiles at the other end of the field before coming out at a junction of roads. Cross over and follow Woodside Road which for most of the way has a pavement on the left-hand side. Where the road narrows take a path on the right side of the road but at the end of the fence, cross the road again and take a public footpath which you will see signed opposite.*

2. *If you are doing the shorter walk you will link up here (see 9 below). Follow a path by the side of some gardens and go over a stile. The path here can sometimes be muddy because of cattle but you should be able to negotiate it if you keep close to the edge. At the end of a field go through a gate or over a stile and make for the next stile into the woods. Cross a little stream and keep straight on at a crossroads of paths. Cross a footbridge over a larger stream and go through a gate. The path keeps straight on uphill to Noddings Farm.*

3. *Before the farm entrance is reached turn right over a stile and about 75 yards ahead take another stile on the right and bear half-left across a field. Cross a footbridge and continue in the same general direction to reach another stile in the field corner. Cross it and go through Kiln Copse. Cross a stile out of a wood and cross the field to a stile by the road.*

4. *After crossing the road take a path diagonally to the right by the tennis courts. Continue over a stile and pass along a track by a walking stick factory. Keep straight on by a stream. Soon the path passes close by a house and appears to be part of the garden. Go through a gate and turn right towards railway station.*

5. *For walkers coming by rail this will be the start of the walk. Go past the station car park and Pig 'n' Whistle. Cross the main road by the Witley Station Stores and take the Greensand Way (waymarked GW). On reaching the main road at the end of the path turn left and shortly take a road to the right (taking care in crossing the main road). Where this minor road bears sharply to the right take the sandy path to the left, signposted Public Bridleway (but ignore a further track over to the left). A little further on this bridleway also has the GW marking (ignore the two permissive bridleways going off to the right).*

6. *About 30 yards before reaching the large white house at a junction of six paths, turn left and take the right-hand of the two bridleways. At the next junction take a path marked Public Bridleway which goes off slightly to the right (ignore path turning to left). At the next junction turn right along a bridleway (ignoring the footpath and the next two footpaths that go off to the left). Cross a plank bridge and once out of the wood the path bears right with fields on either side and leads to the road by the Merry Harriers.*

7. *Cross the road and take the footpath opposite the pub. On reaching the narrow road just before the church turn left to see the disused lime kiln. Otherwise, take the second public footpath on the right directly opposite Court Farm and marked GW. The path goes downhill taking a diagonal line across fields. After going over two more stiles turn left at a junction of roads and keep on the upper right-hand of the two.*

8. *At the next junction take the bridleway to the left which goes by some cottages. On reaching the next road cross over and bear right to pick up the bridleway indicated to the left 20 yards ahead. Follow this made up bridleway until you reach the main road. Cross to the pavement on the opposite side and then turn left until you reach the Winterton Arms.*

9. *Those doing the shorter walk should take the path opposite the pub and on reaching the road at the other end pick up the footpath going off to the right (see 2 above).*
    If bound for Chiddingfold, continue along the main road past the Winterton Arms and when you have a clear view of the traffic, cross over to the pub side. Before the bend take the public footpath left by Lincoln's Hill Cottage. Turn right over a stile, keep by the left-hand side of the field, cross a stile and keep straight on where the path crosses another public footpath. The path passes through a line of trees and crosses a field before reaching a road. Turn right and this leads straight back to the green where the car is parked.

Public Transport
You can catch a train to Witley Station on the Guildford – Haslemere line and start the walk from 5 above. Buses also run to Witley Station and Chiddingfold from Guildford and Haslemere.

26

(Variation 3½ miles, easy 2¼ miles)

St Martha's and Chilworth

Outline
St Martha's Hill — Chilworth Manor — Chilworth Gunpowder Mills — St Martha's Hill.

Summary
From the car park climb up sandy St Martha's Hill and then drop down to the Chilworth Gunpowder Mills and the Tillingbourne with its many smaller lakes.

Attractions
This is a very beautiful walk with good views northwards to Newlands Corner and southwards to the wooded Blackheath and the higher Greensand Hills.

On St Martha's Hill (573 ft/175m) stands St Martha's Chapel built 900 years ago but largely rebuilt halfway through the last century, with the old materials in the original Norman style. Away from habitation it is a peaceful spot to have a rest or a picnic on the grass or seats provided on the bracken- and heather-covered hillside. Because of a steep drop down and up from the Tillingbourne valley this is one of the hardest walks in the book. As an alternative, less energetic parents and younger children may like to just continue along the Pilgrim's Way and go on to the Chantries Wood, an open space maintained by Guildford Borough Council. Much of Surrey is now given over to the stabling of horses but on the shorter walk you pass Tytings Farm. This has a variety of animals that may sometimes even include rare breeds.

On the longer walk you pass Chilworth Manor, a 17th and 18th century house built on the site of an 11th century monastery.

You then go on to the site of the Chilworth Gunpowder Mills. The mills were one of the largest in Britain. Powered by the Tillingbourne, they were active from 1625 until 1920. At one period there were some 16 powder mills in the area. Some converted to papermaking but both industries declined and died after the First Great War. You may think that perhaps this was a good thing for in the past besides the pollution there had been many explosions. One in 1736 brought down the tower of St Martha's and another in 1901 killed six people. At the beginning of this stretch of footpath there is a noticeboard telling you how gunpowder was made. Further along there are streams with remains of mill races and large mill stones. Take care not to fall in. From the gunpowder site there is an optional return to the car park but if you continue on the main walk you pass Albury Mill and the beautiful Waterloo Pond before returning on the hillier side of the Tillingbourne to complete the circuit.

Refreshments
By making a slight deviation off the Gunpowder path you could visit the Percy Arms on the A248 in Chilworth.

Route 5

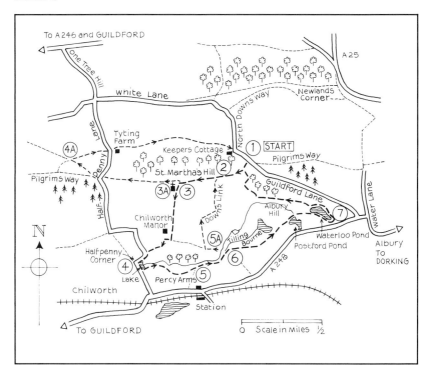

Route 5

St Martha's and Chilworth
4 miles
(Variation 3½ miles, easy 2¼ miles)

Start

From the car park off Guildford Lane, a single track road that leads off the A248 close to a bend in Albury. (Take care not to go up Water Lane which is on the same bend.) (GR 035485). You could also approach from Guildford south of the A246 by taking minor roads, Warren Road, One Tree Hill Road and White Lane (the continuation of Guildford Lane).

Route

1. *From the car park make up the hill, and after a short time the well-marked path bears right.*

2. *Halfway up pass a pill box and the Downs Link path going off to the left. Ignore this and continue up the sandy hill and the church will soon come into view.*

3. *From the churchyard take the gate on the left between the two smallish evergreen trees and go steeply downhill taking care where erosion has exposed rock and water pipes. After the path has levelled out turn right at a T-junction and then turn left on an estate road by Chilworth Manor. Go through lodge gates and continue straight on along the road.*

4. *At Halfpenny Corner the road turns left into Blacksmith Lane and after passing a small lake you will see on the left West Lodge. Go through the iron gate and just inside there is a notice board giving a history of the gunpowder mills. A channelled stream on the right occasionally gushes under the path where at one time there were mill races. Look out for the large mill stones that are by this path.*

5. *About ½ mile along this footpath there is a footbridge on the right that leads to the Percy Arms, station and bus stop. Continuing along the main path you will reach a junction of paths with a ruined gunpowder mill beyond. If you prefer a less steep return take a left-hand path (see 5a below), otherwise continue straight on.*

6. *On reaching the lane turn right, cross the Tillingbourne and almost immediately turn left on the footpath to cross a field diagonally. You will see a lake to the left but you will continue on the path over the stile to Albury Mill, passing left of another lake with some fine Muscovy ducks. You then pass right of Waterloo Pond before coming out on the main road.*

7. *Turn left and almost immediately turn left again at Vale End following footpath signs through the attractive gardens of these houses. The path then bends right*

uphill through some posts. At the junction of paths turn right along the boundary fence of a house. Keeping to the main path you will have views of the Tillingbourne below before climbing the steep hill back to the car park.

Variation

5a. *At the end of the left-hand footpath (5 above) after going through the gate turn left on the same track. This crosses a stream and continues in the same direction until reaching a signpost where you should turn right on the Downs Link. This winds its way up to the pill box at 2 (ignore any paths going off to the left). At the pill box turn right on to the original path back to the car park.*

Shorter, easier walk

3a. *At the church, instead of turning left, continue in the same direction as before on a more gentle downhill path to the road. Cross this and a short distance within the wooded Chantries take the right-hand path downhill.*

4a. *On coming out of the wood turn right on the bridleway. Cross the road (Tytings Farm is on the right) and continue along the bridleway until you reach the road. You can follow this back to the car park, or, if you want to avoid the road, turn right uphill by Keeper's Cottage and take the first left back to the car park.*

Public Transport

Some weekday trains stop at Chilworth Station. The Guildford to Dorking and some other Guildford buses go through Chilworth village. It is a short walk past the Percy Arms to find the lane by the school which leads to the gunpowder path at 5.

St Martha's Hill, with the church on top

30

Newlands Corner and Shere

Outline
Newlands Corner — Hollister Farm — Shere — Tillingbourne Valley —
Silver Wood — Newlands Corner.

Summary
This is a varied walk combining beech woods, open countryside, and a stream where
there are normally a collection of ducks. This is a favourite place for countryside
picnics, with toilets and picnic tables.

Attractions
The North Downs at Newlands Corner reach up to 500 ft (152m) and give good views.
To the south-west can be seen the small church on the top of St Martha's Hill and to
the south-east Albury Park and Shere for which we are bound.

The walk begins on the level along an ancient trackway which is now part of the
North Downs Way. We then take a path which drops down the escarpment to Shere,
one of England's prettiest villages, with many cottages dating from the 17th century.

The church of St James is worth a visit. The shingled spire tops an early Norman
Tower. The nave, the south door and part of the south transept walls are also Norman.
In 1329 with the permission of the Bishop of Winchester, Christine Carpenter
volunteered to be an anchoress and lived as a religious recluse in an enclosed cell on
the north wall of the church. Food was passed to her through a gap in the cell wall.
From this gap she would also watch the service. Just north of the main road and west
of the village is the attractive Silent Pool. This is fed by a chalk spring and contains
deep swallow holes. It is so named because no current is apparent on the surface of
the water despite an ever-flowing spring. Legend has it that King John frightened a
local girl into drowning in the Silent Pool.

The walk continues along the Tillingbourne taking us through the village. Then
after some fields, we climb slightly, on to a greensand ridge. From here we can look
back to the North Downs and see the woodland path which we covered earlier. Finish
by climbing back up the escarpment to Newlands Corner. As well as the large areas
of hawthorn scrub, there are open patches of chalk grassland. In summer these are
covered by many varieties of wild flowers, including orchids, field scabious, rockrose
and marjoram. Many of the flowers are protected and therefore should not be picked.

Refreshments
There is a refreshment kiosk at Newlands Corner. On the other side of the road is a
cafe. In Middle Street, Shere there is Asters Tea Shop (closed Tuesday). In Shere,
the White Horse has a good selection of food but becomes very crowded at weekends.
If there is room children are accepted in the Pilgrim's Bar. The Prince of Wales is
a good alternative.

Route 6

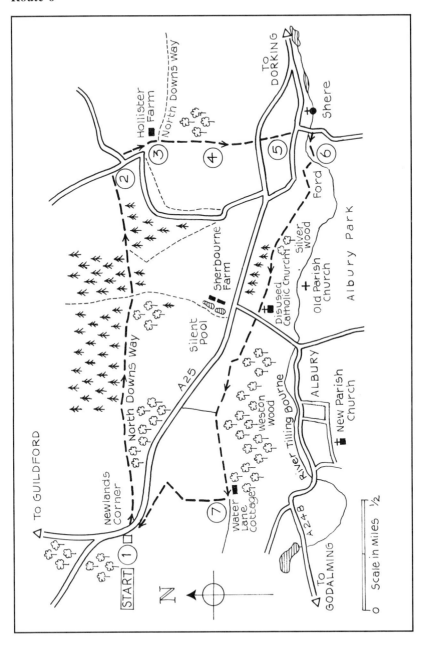

Route 6

Newlands Corner and Shere 5½ miles

Start

At *Newlands Corner Car Park and Picnic Area on the western side of the A25 two miles south of Clandon Station (GR 044493).*

Route

1. On leaving the car park, cross the main road and take the North Downs Way Path (signed by finger posts and stencilled motifs of acorns on gate posts. Follow this eastwards for 1½ miles, ignoring other paths until you reach West Hanger Surrey County Council open space and a narrow tarmac lane.

2. Turn sharp right on this road and after a short distance, turn left at road junction. About 45 yards further on turn on to the track marked Hollister Farm.

3. Follow this track until you see a building on the right (not the farm which is further on to the left). By a finger post marking for the North Downs Way, our path leaves the Way and continues southwards deviating a few yards to the left. This bridleway is clearly marked with a blue arrow on a fallen tree. It then continues in its original southerly direction down the escarpment of the North Downs. To the right of this is a well-walked subsidiary path by a barbed wire fence with open fields and good views to the west and south. This does not appear to be designated, but if you should stray on this, both paths lead to the same spot.

4. The path follows downhill and eventually drops down to a deep gully which leads to a short tunnel under the main road (A25). This path leads direct to Shere village with the sports field on the left-hand side.

5. On reaching the road turn left for a very short distance and then right down Middle Street to the centre of the village. After crossing the River Tillingbourne, turn right along the lane beside the stream.

6. After about 100 yards the road turns right over a ford. Go over the wooden footbridge. A short distance up this road on the left-hand side is the entrance to the old rectory. Take the path which is just to the right of this entrance which soon skirts a brick wall. After crossing a narrow lane the path cuts across a field to Silver Wood. Keeping in the same direction, walk through the wood and more fields. As you approach the road the closed Catholic Apostolic Church of Albury can be seen to the left of the path. Crossing this road, the route continues in the same direction. However if there is time, you could make a detour to see the Silent Pool. To do this turn right along the road, cross the A25 and on the left-hand side by a car park there is a gate clearly marked to the pool. Returning to the original

path cross a field and skirt the northern side of Weston Wood. Ignore the track going off to the right (there is also a house on the left-hand side) but continue in the same direction where the path has now changed to a cart track.

7. *Just past the next habitation (Water Lane Cottages) on the left-hand side, turn right. At the next farm the path bears to the right and then to the left uphill, back to Newlands Corner car park, with the main road above you.*

Public Transport
Newlands Corner has been picked as the start of the walk because of its large car park. Only the odd bus goes that way but the walk can be started just as conveniently from Shere (5 on the walk). Buses run regularly from Guildford to Dorking and a few go from Guildford elsewhere.

Leith Hill Tower

34

Friday Street and Leith Hill

Outline
Friday Street − Broadmoor − Coldharbour − Leith Hill − Abinger Bottom − Friday Street.

Summary
This is an interesting circular walk covering some of Surrey's finest scenery. After a rainy period it may be difficult to avoid the odd stretch of mud but most of the walk is over dry greensand and can be undertaken any time of the year. Paths that go through extensive woods are not always signposted; so due care will need to be taken to look out for changes of direction in the walk.

Attractions
Friday Street is an isolated hamlet just south of a small lake in a steep wooded valley. It is a very popular place in summer. There is no public transport. By car, the approach is along single track lanes cutting through high sandstone banks. The large car park lies at the top of the hill above the western side of the lake. The Stephen Langton Inn is named after an Archbishop of Canterbury who was born in this area and helped to persuade King John to sign the Magna Carta in 1215.

Broadmoor on the shorter walk is an even smaller hamlet but again is an attractive wooded valley close to the source of the Tillingbourne. Beyond on the southern edge of the Leigh Hill escarpment is Coldharbour. To the eastern edge of this hill is the prehistoric site of Anstlebury, an ancient hill fort. Later in history Ethelwulf the West Saxon king, defeated the invading Danes just south of here in 851.

From Coldharbour there is an easy climb to Leith Hill. At the summit (967ft/ 294m) we have the highest point in the south-east of England. On a clear day if the tower is open (see refreshments) it is well worth climbing the spiral staircase. Part of the way up there is a room with a National Trust display of the locality. At the top of the tower there is a very good view above the pine trees. London can be seen to the north and in the opposite direction the South Downs. If you are lucky you may even see the sea through the Shoreham Gap.

The return is downhill through the woods to Abinger Bottom and the stream, which leads back to Friday Street and its picturesque lake.

Refreshments
At Leith Hill Tower there is a refreshment kiosk which is open 2 pm to 5 pm every weekend throughout the year, Bank Holiday Mondays, Boxing Day and New Year's Day, and Wednesdays from end of March to end of September. There are picnic tables outside the Plough in Coldharbour, and a beer garden at the Stephen Langton in Friday Street.

Route 7

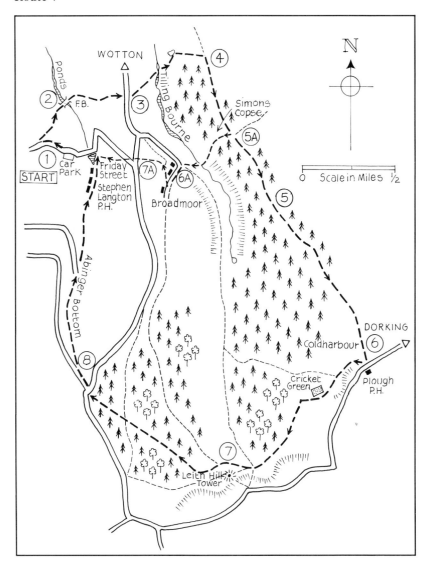

Route 7

Friday Street and Leith Hill

6 miles
(Variation 2½ miles)

Start

At Friday Street car park on the western side of the hamlet (GR 127457). This can be reached by following the narrow lanes south of the A25, either by the Wotton Hatch Hotel or by going another ½ mile towards Guildford and taking the next road signposted Wotton and Leith Hill. About 1½ miles south take a sharp left turning down a single track lane for the car park.

Route

1. *From the car park turn left along the path above the road and follow this for about ¼ mile. On the right-hand side of the road there are some white gates. Take the path which goes by these gates doubling back from the original direction of the road down to a valley. Near the bottom just before the entrance to a cottage, turn right at footpath sign with a field on the left-hand side. Shortly a series of hammer ponds or fish ponds come into view.*

2. *After crossing a bridge by one of these ponds and a stile, the path climbs steeply up a sandy hillside. At the top of the hill, the path straight on is marked private and the right of way bears slightly to the left. It then bears right with a small field on the right-hand side. (Ignore the path going sharply left).*

3. *The path crosses a narrow road and continues to the bottom of the hill with a causeway over a pond. Turn left a short distance further on along a track. Just beyond the next pond on the left there is a path on the right. This path goes gently up the hill by the side of the field.*

4. *At the top of the field turn right along a path which has been churned up by horses and motor bicycles. (Where fallen trees allow there is a drier path running parallel just above this.)*

5. *The main track bears slightly to the left and about ¼ mile further on you reach a crossroads of paths where those doing the shorter variation turn off to the right (see 5a). The principal path continues in a south-easterly direction for nearly 2 miles, the track eventually coming out at Coldharbour with the Plough on the opposite side of the road.*

6. *In Coldharbour, on the same side of the road as you entered the hamlet, a track goes up the hill by a few cottages. Follow this track, which passes left of a cricket green. Just after this, take the left-hand fork continuing up the hill. At a dip in the ground continue roughly in the same direction, ignoring the path that runs through*

the hollow. After a further short climb, Leith Hill Tower will be spotted immediately ahead.

7. On leaving the Tower continue in the same direction as you were going previously, ignoring the well-worn path on the right. After about a hundred yards take a similar path going off diagonally to the right. This leads down to a road junction where the right-hand turn is signposted to Broadmoor.

8. Cross the road and just past this turn take a path on the right which gradually descends to Abinger Bottom. Keep now in the same direction all the way down to the valley. When you reach the surfaced lane take it for about 50 yards but look out for the path which restarts on the right-hand side. The path soon follows a stream all the way down to Friday Street. Beyond the Stephen Langton the road leads to the lake. The car park is up the hill on the left.

Variation
Follow the walk from 1 above to the turn off mentioned at 5.

5a. Turn right when you reach a crossroads of paths and follow the right-hand side of a bracken clearing in a wooded area and then descend through an area known as Simons Copse. At a junction of paths drop down a step and continue in the same direction down a path in a gully. About 50 yards after crossing two small streams with a cottage through the woods there is a path through the trees on the right which cuts the corner, regaining the track near the junction, to the made up road through Broadmoor. There are some stables on the other side of the road.

6a. Turn left along this road and three cottages further on a footpath goes up the hill on the right by entrance No. 7. Keep straight on uphill (ignore path on right). At the top there are a number of paths. Aim for the one which keeps in the same direction. This comes out at the top of the eastern junction to the road going back to Friday Street.

7a. Cross this junction (keeping to the left of the Friday Street road) and turn right down the hill through the wood. Look out for a wider path coming down the hill on the right near the NT sign and join this. The lake will come into view at the bottom and the car park is just up the hill on the other side of the valley.

Public Transport
On the longer walk you may be able to start from Coldharbour (6 on walk) if you select on weekdays the occasional postal bus from Dorking or on summer Sundays and bank holidays the circular bus from Guildford which calls at Dorking Station.

Ranmore Common (Dogkennel Green End)

Outline
Ranmore — Yewtree Farm — Effingham Golf Course — Oldlands Wood.

Summary
This is an interesting North Downs walk through sheep pastures, with beach woods to explore and good views to the north.

Attractions
Start this walk from the western end of Ranmore Common, 500 acres of National Trust woodland. Later on the walk, by Yewtree Farm you will see Polsden Lacey through the trees. This is one of the great NT houses of Surrey. The NT also own more land on the southern slopes of this part of the North Downs with other car parks closer to hand. The NT book, *Walks in the Home Counties* details a good walk covering much of their own area. Our walk goes further westwards through a variety of woodland rich in flowers and open downland with many grazing sheep and other farm animals. Deep in the woods east of this walk is the ancient and well-used Tanners Hatch Youth Hostel. By the car park there is sufficient space to picnic and play games. Also, if the family tire, they could be left at the refreshment spot whilst the driver collects the car.

Refreshments
On the walk we go past the Ranmore Arms public house which has a children's play house and climbing frame. Next door is the Old Cart Lodge Tea House and across the road another house which advertises teas.

Public Transport
There is no regular service to Ranmore. There are two buses for shoppers on Friday morning. There is also a vintage circular bus from Guildford that runs three times a day on summer Sundays and Public Holidays which calls at Polsden Lacey and Dorking.

Route 8

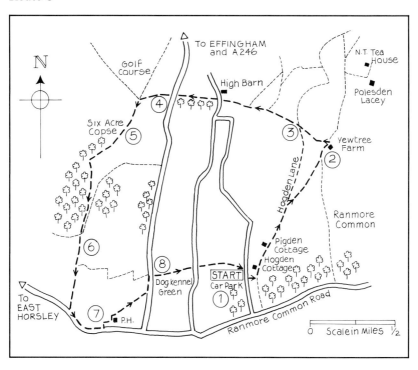

Route 8

Ranmore Common (Dogkennel Green End)

4¾ miles
(Variation 2 miles)

Start

The best approach is to take the Ranmore Road from the A2003 (the Dorking bypass road on the northern side between the A24 and A25). After climbing the hill and passing the road from Ranmore church, our road is about a mile ahead on the right with the car park a short way down on the left (GR 124504).

Route

1. *From car park entrance cross the road and take the path opposite. About 50 yards ahead there is a waymarked NT post. Turn left on a wider track. Where the wood on the right finishes, cross a stile and take a footpath diagonally across the field. At the top of the hill turn left by the fence. At the end of the field cross the stile and turn left along a stony track.*

2. *By Yew Tree Farm turn sharp left. (Just as you turn left you can see Polsden Lacey through the trees on the right). Further on, where the track bends right, take the stile on the left of this bend and cut across the field to join the track in the valley after crossing another stile.*

3. *Turn right on this track and 25 yards ahead turn left on the bridleway along the edge of a field. Take the right-hand fork where the path divides and at a meeting of tracks continue along a narrow path with a field on the left. (There is a bridleway just to the right running parallel with our path.) On reaching a metalled road cross over slightly to the right and you will see a footpath continuing in the same direction as before. Continue across another metalled road and at the end of the boundary hedge of a large garden you reach Effingham Golf Course.*

4. *Take care of the golfers. The path cuts across the golf course going slightly to the left, making for the copse of trees. Skirt this and cut across the fairway where two black and white posts can be seen. Walk along the upper copse until a marked public footpath to the left comes into view.*

5. *Follow this path into Six Acre Copse, crossing two indistinct junctions of paths. The path then bears left still in the wood but along the edge of the field.*

6. *At a junction of paths by a bungalow turn left. The path soon comes into the open, passing a large house on the left. The track is now tarmac up to the main road. Turn left on this and, after a bend in the road, turn left at the Old Cart Lodge Tea Rooms.*

7. *The path turns right before the entrance and goes round the back of the pub (to get to the front you will need to turn to the right). Behind the buildings the path goes over a stile and cuts across two fields to a small wood. Cross the stile and take the left-hand path through this copse.*

8. *On reaching the road turn right for about 25 yards and a footpath sign can be seen on the other side. Go up the hill, crossing the stile near the top, and continue straight on, joining a track. Cross the road, and continue on the track on the other side. Where this bends to the right continue on the footpath and at the top of the hill the car park is on the right.*

Variation

Those who only wish to do a short walk can return to the car park by turning left in the valley, at the end of 2 above. This is a continuation of the original lane.

An ancient lane onto the White Downs, guarded by a ghostly World War II pillbox

3¾ miles
(Variation 1¾ miles)

Norbury Park and Fetcham Downs

Outline
Fetcham − Bocketts Farm − Norbury Park (close to House) −
Roaringhouse Farm − The Hazels − Fetcham.

Summary
This is a walk through wooded Norbury Park and the fringing area of farmland, with
some magnificent rural landscapes of the Mole Valley. There are a few hills to climb
but most of the paths are on the level.

Attractions
This walk is through the Norbury Park estate, the first area of countryside to be
purchased by Surrey County Council in 1931. Norbury Park House with 40 acres of
land was sold off a year later and is still in private ownership. The house was built
in 1774 by William Locke and since then has changed hands many times.

This has always been one of my favourite areas. As a child I have happy memories
of visiting my grandfather, who lived in Great Bookham, and wandering over Fetcham
Downs with other children. We had favourite trees to climb and where farm tractors
had made rutted tracks we pretended we were going up and down in steam trains.

On this walk we start by following a track down to Bocketts Farm which caters
for children. In addition to a variety of farm animals there is a barn with rescued
creatures from other parts of the world such as snakes and birds of prey.

Leaving the farm land we go into the woods. Some areas were badly affected by
the Great Storm of 1987. A lot of replanting has been carried out and on our path in
Updown Wood you will come across yew and beech sculptures carved out of some
of the old trees. 'Trefoil' by Steve Geliot is particularly interesting.

Coming down the hill just before Roaringhouse Farm you will see a small wooden
barn built on concrete mushroom stilts. Many old barns were built like this to prevent
rodents getting into the stored crops. We then climb up the hill along a covered
bridleway by the side of an area carpeted with primroses in the early spring. In the
past this woodland was coppiced regularly (cut down to just above ground level and
allowed to regrow) to provide bean and pea sticks and wattle fencing. After leaving
these larger trees, still good cover for nesting birds, we go past some fields back to
the main road.

Refreshments
The Old Barn Tea Rooms at Bocketts Farm is open for coffee, lunches, cream teas,
ice-cream, and other snacks.

Route 9

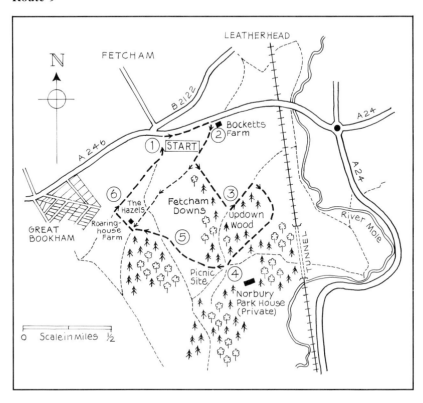

Route 9

Norbury Park and Fetcham Downs

3¾ miles
(Variation 1¾ miles)

Start

The walk starts from the Fetcham car park at the top of Young Street. This is the southern part of the Leatherhead by-pass A246 (GR 152549). If on the walk you intend to visit Bocketts Farm you could start from the large car park there. Leave the main road by the same Fetcham roundabout but take the farm track parallel with that road (GR 155550).

Route

1. On leaving the car park make for the farm road going down hill by the side of Young Street. There is also a bridleway going the same way to Bocketts Farm but this may be too rough for children at some times of the year.

2. At Bocketts Farm turn right and just beyond the field on the left, turn left on the marked public footpath into the woods. The path gradually climbs a hill, and at a junction of three paths take a left-hand one closest to the field.

3. At the next junction turn sharp left. A good view of Leatherhead and the north-west can be seen before the cinder track turns right. Our next view is down the Mole Valley on the left. You leave the bridleway where this turns left and keep straight on past the timber sculptures.

4. Duck under the access gate and, on reaching the metalled road, if you look through the fence you will see Norbury Park House. Turn right and on your left you will see picnic tables and a noticeboard giving details and a history of the area. Take the right-hand bridleway and at the first signpost keep on this main track ignoring any tracks to the right. The path becomes stony as it drops down between trees.

5. Cross the wide track in the valley and climb the bridleway on the other side. Then descend a short steep hill to Roaringhouse Farm. Go past the farm cottages and at a junction of paths at the top of the hill turn right on to a bridleway.

6. To the right of this path is 'The Hazels' plantation. On reaching the open farmland turn left at the junction and this track leads back to the car park.

Shorter variation

After leaving Bocketts Farm (2), instead of leaving the main path continue to the end where there is a junction of paths, and turn left along a valley through the downs. This would be a good spot to picnic and play. At the next junction of paths you turn right and at this spot you will have rejoined the main walk at (5).

Public Transport

Both the Kingston – Leatherhead – Dorking – Horsham bus and weekdays the Croydon – Leatherhead – Guildford bus runs up the B2122 to the roundabout close to the starting point. On summer Sunday afternoons the Surrey Hills leisure bus Gatwick, Dorking to Leatherhead rail station also calls at Bocketts Farm.

The latest arrivals at Bocketts Farm

46

Headley and Walton-on-the-Hill

Outline
Headley Heath – Walton-on-the-Hill – Frith Farm – Headley Heath.

Summary
This is an interesting walk over rolling countryside. Starting on acid soil the track is soon on chalk with patches of Surrey clay and loam.

Attractions
Headley is a commuter village within the London Green Belt. Headley Heath and the Lordship of the Manor were given to the National Trust in 1946. In the Second World War the Heath was used as a tank training ground by the Canadian Army. The disturbance encouraged birch to grow but in recent years the NT have encouraged the re-establishment of heather.

Cricket is regularly played on summer weekends whilst the Heath is popular with people exercising their dogs and horses confined to the bridle paths.

The National Trust have a ramble over the Heath and Box Hill in their *Walks in the Home Counties* book. Our walk is to the east of this NT area. We leave the heath for farmland mainly used for grazing horses. As you leave the village, Epsom grandstand can be seen in the middle distance. At the corner of Queen's Close in Walton-on-the-Hill is an aquarium selling many varieties of tropical fish. In the same area to the north of this walk, there is a village pond with ducks and swans.

Refreshments
The refreshments hut by the car park provides a good selection of snacks and also maps of the area. A short distance off the walk (by the church in the village) the Cock provides meals and snacks. During the summer, refreshments are sometimes available in the village hall.

Route 10

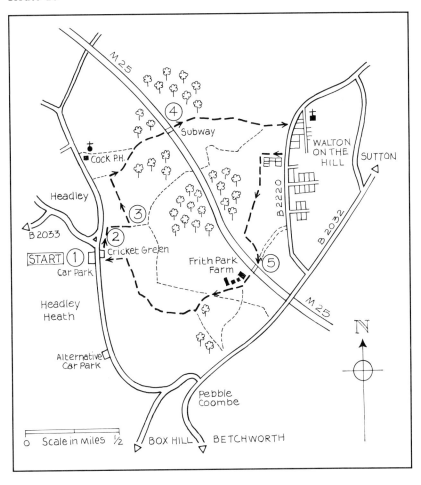

Route 10

Headley and Walton-on-the-Hill   4 miles

Start

From Headley Heath (NT) main car park. This is just south of Headley village on the west side of the B2033, 3½ miles south east of Leatherhead (GR 205538). (If this is full there is another car park about half a mile south of this.)

Route

1. *From the car park cross the road to the north side of the cricket green and follow a path running parallel with the road for about ¼ mile.*

2. *Where the path almost meets the road there is a drive to the right. Take this and when the house gates are reached the path continues around the left-hand side of the grounds.*

3. *About ¼ mile further on at a field boundary take a left-hand footpath. The path continues in a straight line crossing a field boundary, a drive and another field boundary before reaching a track crossing at right angles. Turn right down this track and, after about a quarter of a mile, go through a bluebell wood and under the subway of the M25.*

4. *From the motorway follow a bridle track up hill and take a right hand path to Queen's Close, Walton-on-the-Hill. Turn right on the B2220 (passing The Chequer's, a large pub on the left-hand side of the road). On the right-hand side, past Bramley School, take a path by a housing estate. At the end of the houses turn left by a recreation ground. Go into the narrow belt of woodland and out to the right where the path crosses diagonally over farmland and then sharp left to come out by the stables on Love Lane,*

5. *Turn right and after crossing the bridge over the M25 go round the left-hand side of Frith Park Farm. (Keep close to the farm, ignoring another path going off to the left). At the next junction of paths take the left turning through a wood and, at the next T-junction turn right. At the top of the hill take any of the paths going off to the left. The cricket ground and the car park will soon come into sight.*

An archway from the old church of St Mary the Virgin, Headley

Bottom Branstead Wood, a view from the car park

Banstead Wood and Downs

Outline
Car Park – Banstead Wood – Fames Rough – Perrott Farm – Park Downs – Car Park.

Summary
A circular walk skirting Banstead Wood with good views of open downland, or a shorter walk coming back on another path through the wood.

Attractions
The 250-acre Banstead Wood is one of the largest areas of Special Scientific Interest (SSI's) in Surrey and is owned by Reigate and Banstead Council. The mixed woodland is covered in bluebells in the spring and is traversed by an extensive network of paths from which you may be able to identify some of the many birds nesting in the area. These include woodpeckers and owls. Wild rhododendrons, a native of the Himalaya, are becoming a nuisance because the chemicals in their decaying leaves discourage the propagation of native trees. Efforts are being made to reduce their numbers. Despite this problem, on the shorter walk which cuts through the edge of the wood you will be able to see very large specimens of oak and beech trees. On both walks, looking down from the path towards the railway is Fames Rough, an area of rough grassland important for its flora. On the longer walk, after going through varied farmland you reach Park Downs. This has a mixture of hawthorne and grassland with many wild flowers. Once again this is an area full of birds including most members of the warbler family.

Refreshments
There is a tea and ice-cream hut close to the car park which is open most weekends of the year other than the worst of the winter months.

Route 11

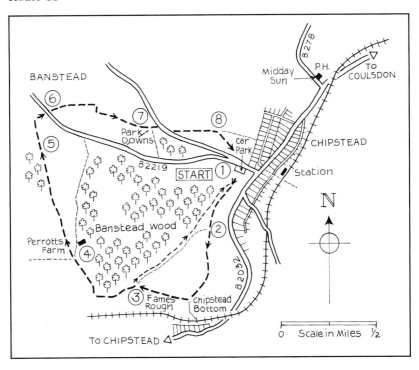

Route 11

Banstead Wood and Downs

4 miles
(Variation 2 miles)

Start

From Banstead take the B2219 to Chipstead. The large car park (GR 274583) is on the right-hand side just before the road junction. If approaching from the B2032 turn into the road signposted to Banstead (left from Kingswood or right from Coulsdon and Woodmansterne).

Route

1. *From the car park take either of the gates each side of the toilets with your back to the road. The paths soon join and go over open grassland. Keep to the path just outside the wood.*

2. *Where the tracks divide keep straight on, ignoring the path on the right going uphill. When you reach the field, the path keeps to the top edge of the field with views to the left across the Chipstead Valley. At the end of the field, don't drop downhill, turn right into a narrow wood, then left following the well marked path in previous general direction.*

3. *After going through a beech grove you arrive at a T-junction of paths. This is where the variation separates from the main walk. Turn left to follow the 4 mile walk. At the end of the level path, it bears right uphill. You cross a stile into a field and the path then keeps close to the side of the wood.*

4. *Cross the stile at Perrotts Farm and continue in the same direction through the farm gate (or the stile when this is shut). There is a public footpath sign here. Ignore the bridleway just to the right-hand side of this. When the farm track turns left, our grassy track continues in the original direction. At the end of this field there is a wood. Immediately before reaching it, turn right over a stile into another field and then turn left to continue by the edge of the wood in the same direction as previously.*

5. *Cross the stile at the end of the fields and at the crossroads of footpaths on the other side, take the path which goes slightly uphill through the woods maintaining the same direction as before. The well trodden path then wanders to the right until it reaches the road.*

6. *Cross the service road and take care crossing the main road to the stile opposite. Follow the path along the edge of the field. At the end of the field the path turns right. About 50 yards ahead it then turns left over another stile and goes through scrubland. After a short distance take the right-hand path to join a lower path but continue in the same direction. The path is now once again on the open downs.*

7. At the next junction of paths, take the path slightly to the right but keep on the same contour, avoiding other paths to the right or left. Now take care crossing a road and there is a footpath directly opposite through the woods. Fifty yards ahead take the left-hand path, still continuing in the same direction.

8. About 500 yards ahead follow the first path on the right going diagonally downhill. At the moment, there is a sycamore tree at the corner and a fallen tree in view down the hill. Follow this path through the beechwood. Ignore the first meeting of paths but at the T-junction turn right. The car park can be seen just across the two roads. (If you miss the sycamore tree it does not matter, you can continue to the end of the path where the backs of gardens can be seen. Turn right, and the path leads back to the car park).

Variation
At 3, turn right and go into Banstead Wood. Just inside the wood, turn right on a track made of disused roadstone and follow this straight to the car park, ignoring any grass tracks on either side of the path.

Public Transport
Trains from Victoria (Charing Cross Sundays) to Tattenham Corner call at Chipstead Station. Epsom buses run from Epsom to West Croydon and stop by the Midday Sun in the Chipstead Valley. This is a short walk from the car park. Selhurst bus starts from the same pub and runs to East Croydon and Shirley. Both buses go via Coulsdon and Purley.

Chipstead Valley

5 miles
(Variation 4¼ miles)

Reigate Hill and Gatton Park

Outline
Reigate Hill — Crossways Farm — Old Mint House — Gatton Bottom —
Gatton Park — Reigate Hill.

Summary
Despite straddling a motorway this walk covers a beautiful area, well worth a visit
with a mixture of woodland, copses and mixed farming.

Attractions
The walk starts from Reigate Hill car park on a sharp escarpment looking down on
the towns of Reigate and Redhill. Several miles of this very attractive part of the North
Downs are here owned by the National Trust, but the area is now rather hemmed in
by the M25 which crosses a number of footpaths. Fortunately the motorway is in a
cutting from where we begin our walk.

As we make our way eastward and downhill through the woods of the National
Trust part of Gatton Park, the motorway comes into view. We go underneath this just
where the cutting changes to an embankment. North of the M25 we climb a country
lane where you may be able to see pheasants darting in and out of the undergrowth.

The walk then passes through open dairy farmland to a private property called the
Old Mint House. Could this have been an area where in the past peppermint was
distilled? We then make our way back downhill to Gatton Bottom, returning to Reigate
Hill through Gatton Park. At one time it was a rotten borough which before the 1832
Reform Act returned two MPs from a local population drawn from twenty-three
houses. Now the park houses the Royal Alexandra and Albert co-ed boarding school.
We wind our way close to the buildings and playing fields before returning to the
National Trust woods. On many sections of the walk there are beautiful views of the
area. Other than from the car park it would be hard to believe that there was a built
up area close at hand.

Refreshments
There is a kiosk cafe in the car park which is open every day except for two or three
weeks around Christmas time. There are other eating places in Reigate.

Route 12

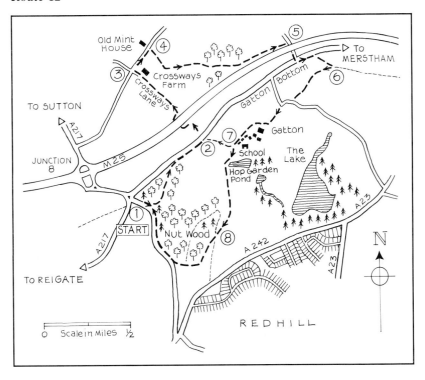

Route 12

Reigate Hill and Gatton Park

5 miles
(Variation 4¼ miles)

Start

From the car park at the top of Reigate Hill. From Junction 8 M25 roundabout take the A217 to Reigate and at the next junction turn left onto the Mersham Road, but immediately turn right by car park sign (GR 263523).

Route

1. *From the eastern side of the car park cross the road and take the North Downs path through Gatton Park for about 20 yards but then turn left, (you will rejoin the long distance path lower down the hill).*

2. *At the bottom of the hill turn left on a made-up road. Go through lodge gates, take care crossing the road and proceed up a lane on the opposite side of the road to the M25. The lane does a loop to the left to get under the motorway and then continues uphill in the original direction along Crossways Lane. If you are lucky you may spot some pheasants.*

3. *At a crossroads just past Crossways Farm turn right on a lane marked High Road.*

4. *About ¼ mile ahead on the left is the Old Mint House and shortly afterwards on the right a public footpath is signposted. Cross a stile and another about 25 yards ahead on the left-hand side of a field, then proceed in the same direction along a hedge on the right-side of a field. After crossing another stile, continue along farm track until this bears to the left. You will see a stile on the right. Cross this, and continue alongside the hedge in the same direction as the lane, going over two more stiles and then on the left going by the edge of a wood. At the corner of the field (where another wood continues on the right) go over a stile and continue downhill through the wood. On reaching farmland proceed along the edge of the wood to the motorway. The path continues through a field between the M25 and a small copse and then through another small belt of woodland.*

5. *Ahead you will see a gate. Cross a stile and turn right on the road to get under the M25. At a T-junction turn left onto Gatton Bottom and about 100 yards ahead turn right on a marked footpath which bears across the field diagonally.*

6. *On meeting the North Downs Way (lined with trees) turn right. Further on, by some houses this path turns to a track, and when this becomes made up it bears left and then right (finger posts help to mark the way). The path then goes through the entrance of the Royal Alexandra and Albert School. After passing a modern chapel the road bears to the right (with school buildings on the left).*

7. At the end of the buildings the road bears round to the right, take the bridleway which goes roughly straight on. The Hop Garden Pond can be spied through the trees but you will keep to the right of this.

8. At the fork, take the right-hand path, and where the main track bears to the right continue straight on. The path then bears round to the right with a road following round some distance below. When the bridleway goes to the right again, keep straight on, going round the edge of a fence, and pick up another bridleway which dips for a short distance before continuing uphill. At a junction of paths continue straight on. (At this spot to the right, across the downland field, the school can be seen in the hollow below). The path soon takes us back to the starting point.

Shorter variation
Follow the route to 7, but then continue on the road which bears round to the right. Just before the ledge gates, turn left on the path you originally came down. But at a fork, instead of taking the right-hand path, take the left, and at the top of the hill bear round to the right and the car park.

Public Transport
Buses from Raynes Park via Sutton to Reigate and others from Kingston via Epsom to Crawley are on the main road at Reigate Hill close to the car park.

Reigate Heath

58

3½ miles
(Longer variation 6 miles)

Reigate Heath

Outline
Reigate Heath − Skimmington − Reigate Park − Reigate Heath.

Extension
Skimmington − Trumpet's Hill − Ricebridge Farm − Wonham Mill − Dungates Farm − Reigate Heath.

Summary
The main walk is on sandstone and is thus a good dry ramble at any time of the year. The extension of the walk is again mainly on sand but after rain the land can be a bit claggy close to the River Mole.

Attractions
The walk starts on Reigate Heath, common land of about 130 acres. On the heath you should keep your eye out for golfers, for some of the paths and bridleways straddle a 9 hole public course. For much of the walk there are good views north towards the North Downs and at the top of Reigate Park the low-lying Weald can be seen to the south. Ducks and geese frequent Priory Pond.

On the longer variation there are some interesting old farmhouses and more wildfowl on Wonham mill pond. On a quiet day you may be lucky to get a chance sighting of a fleet-footed deer. On returning to the heath some of you who still have the energy may like to explore the seven Bronze Age barrows, marked tumuli on the map, which lie to the north west of the car park. They range in diameter from 24 to 100 feet. Four were excavated early in the 19th century. The largest and one nearby produced some evidence that they were used for cremation burials.

Above the car park to the west lies an old windmill built in 1765. After operating for over a hundred years it was converted into a chapel. Probably most of you will be content to just look at the mill from the outside. It is still in excellent condition with a fine set of sails now fixed and a tailpole which previously turned the mill into the wind. Services are held in the chapel at 3 pm on the third Sunday in the month from May to October. At other times keys may be obtained from the nearby golf house.

Refreshments
The walk passes the friendly Skimmington Castle. The pub has a children's room and picnic tables outside. On Sundays food is limited to such things as Cornish pasties and sausages but there is a good selection of dishes for the remainder of the week. Nearby the town of Reigate has numerous pubs and other eating places.

Route 13

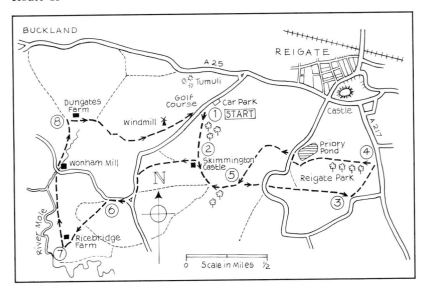

Route 13

Reigate Heath
3½ miles
(Longer variation 6 miles)

Start

Turn south-west off the A25 by the Black Horse. The car park is on both sides of the road a ¼ mile down the lane (GR 239503).

Route

1. *On south-eastern side of the car park follow a well-trodden path into the wood and bear right on the track which goes past two houses and then on to the little hamlet of Skimmington. The path goes by the left-hand side of Skimmington Castle and joins the Greensand Way (GW). The bridleway bears left and joins Littleton Lane.*

2. *At the top of this metalled road cross over the road junction and go up the steps on the right side of the hill. Continue to the top, then follow the ridge east.*

3. *At the other end there is a stone seat. Continue down the hill and near the bottom, just before the road, turn left along a tarmac path.*

4. *Just before the main road turn left again and follow the path through the wood above a playing field. Descend on the path to Priory Pond and go round the western end. Just before the bridge, take the path close to the laurels. Go across the road and follow the path by a stream. At the end of the allotments the path bears left by the edge of a barbed wire fence back to the road. Turn right on the road.*

5. *You can now re-trace your route back to the car park to complete the 3½ mile walk. **For the Longer Variation** re-trace your steps only as far as Skimmington Castle (2). Here take the path by the right-hand side of the front of the pub as you face it. As you come out of the path between some gardens on to a metalled road, turn left on GW and after crossing another quiet metalled road the path leads down to a house where you cut across the left-hand side of the front lawn. The path then leads down to a busier road. Turn left but at the next road junction turn right down Trumpets Hill Road.*

6. *Turn left for Little Santon Farm but almost immediately turn left down a footpath. This joins a farm road continuing in the same direction.*

7. *Just beyond Ricebridge Farm turn right. The path goes due north close by the River Mole. Cross the narrow bridge and turn left on the road. Then turn right by the left-hand side of the mill building. Round the back you will be able to see mallards and tufted ducks on the lake by the old mill house. Cross the fields by a path that comes out to the left of Dangates Farm.*

61

8. *Turn right on the farm road and after going through a small belt of trees turn right through a gate. At a T-junction of paths turn left and quickly right up hill to the windmill. You will see the road and your starting point ahead but below you.*

Public Transport
A bus running from Dorking to Redhill passes the Black Horse at the top of the road where the walk starts. Many more buses and trains go to Reigate where you could join the walk at (4) from Bell Street.

Outwood Windmill

Outwood Mill

Outline
Outwood − Lodge Farm − Horne − Outwood.

Summary
This is an interesting walk in the Weald with good views northwards to the sand ridge around Bletchingley and southwards to wooded Sussex and Turners Hill.

Attractions
This walk starts on the National Trust's Outward Common. A good spot for picnics and playing in the woods. Most of the bridleways are well-made with old road material but being on the clay lands of the Weald some of the ploughed fields can be claggy after wet weather. The open countryside in a northerly direction is a good spot for seeing light aircraft flying towards Redhill airport and to the south jets bound for Gatwick.

You pass the Outwood Swan Sanctuary and Lodge Farm which has a large flock of milk sheep kept for making cheese and yoghurt. Over the crossroads from where you started is the Outwood Windmill. This is the oldest working windmill in England. The post mill was built in 1665 and restored in 1952. With the use of the tailpole the whole mill can be turned to face the wind and when in position the step can be lowered to act as an anchor. The mill with a small museum and a few farm animals is open Easter to October on Sunday and Bank Holidays from 2 pm to 6 pm.

Refreshments
At The Bell close to the start of the walk, emphasis is very much on food, with many set tables reserved for diners. The Dog and Duck just off our map to the west allows children in their restaurant.

Route 14

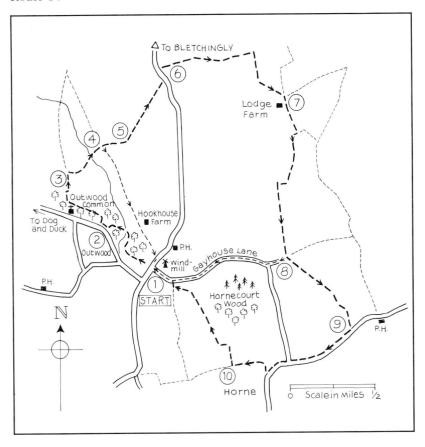

Route 14

Outwood Mill
6 miles
(Shorter variations 5¼ miles and 1¾ miles)

Start

Outwood lies south of the A25. The turning is at a crossroads in the centre of Bletchingley. The car park is down a short track on the south eastern side of Outwood Common with the windmill on the other side of the crossroads (GR 327456). Alternatively you can reach the common by turning off the A23 on the northern side of Salfords. After going over the M23 you turn left at the T junction and turn right just past the Dog and Duck pub. At the end of the road turn left and the car park track is left again.

Route

1. *Continue west from the car park along the track which leads past the cricket green. At the gates just before the pavilion turn left down a hollow. After 25 yards turn right, keeping above the house and stream which are on the left. 300 yards further on through the woods go over a narrow footbridge slightly to the left. This leads to a slightly wider footbridge. Continue straight on up the rise.*

2. *This leads back to the road. Turn right and walk along the verge then by the NT sign turn right back into the wood. Fifty yards on at a T-junction of paths turn left. Ignore the path on the right and go through a horse barrier. On reaching some cottages, cross the track leading to one of these but turn right on the next one (Little Elm Cottage is on the right of this path).*

3. *On coming out of the wood go over a stile and turn right along the edge of the field. Northwards you can now see the sandy ridge near Bletchingley. At the bottom of the field go over a stile, footbridge and then another stile into the next field, continuing in the same direction.*

4. *If you are doing the longer walks, ignore the path crossing this (about ⅔ across the field) but if you are doing the amble turn right and this path leads straight back to the common with the starting point just to your right.*

5. *After going over a stile in the next field, the path cuts diagonally to the left and keeps this direction across the next three fields.*

6. *You come out on the road by the Outwood Swan Sanctuary. Turn left and a short distance along the road turn right along a bridleway. Over the hedge you should be able to see a large collection of swans and geese. A path goes into the wood on the left and shortly after our path cuts across the field on the right with a small pond at the other end by the boundary hedge. This then becomes a made-up path.*

65

Follow this along the edge of the next two fields after which the path bears right along the hedgerows and then goes left into another field. In these fields you may be lucky and see a large flock of milking ewes.

7. *Turn right along the concrete track by Lodge Farm. After reaching another field, the track turns right and then left along a hedgerow. At the end of this field, the track turns right, left again, and continues to a cross road of paths before a copse.*

8. *At the copse the track turns right. If you wish to shorten your walk you can continue that way and follow Gayhouse Lane back to the windmill.*
    On the main walk continue straight on over a narrow bridge, cross a ditch, and come out of the trees to go diagonally left across the next two fields. Continue across the next field aiming for a stile to the right of a house. Go over this and follow round the paddock fence, turning right and continuing on the track down to a made-up road.

9. *Turn right along the road taking care of traffic. In Church Road, Horne, shortly before the bend turn right into a field and there is a made-up path by a hedge on the edge of the road. Before this turns back to the road take the footpath to the right by the edge of the field and go left through the hedge where there is a notice that the path has been diverted by statutory order.*

10. *Turn right at the end of the field and where the field is at its narrowest point, cut across to the other side, making for the wood. Go into the wood. At the top of the hill, when the windmill can be seen the path bears to the left across a field. At the end turn right on the track and then left on the road for the crossroads and car park.*

Public Transport
The odd bus runs from Redhill to Lingfield and Dormansland. You would need to get off and walk down Brickfield Lane close to the Dog and Duck in Outwood and take the first public footpath on Outwood Common. This will lead up to 3 on the walk. Also the Redhill Post Bus goes to Outwood Post Office which is close to the windmill.

2¾ miles
(Variation 2¼ miles)

Godstone and Leigh Place Pond

Outline

Godstone — Churchtown — Leigh Place — Godstone.

Summary

This walk explores mixed woodland with stretches of water alive with wildfowl.

Attractions

Godstone lies on the A25 and an old Roman road just south of the North Downs. The village is centered around a pond and green where cricket and football are played. Close to the pond are three old inns. The White Hart is said to date from Richard II but the oldest identifiable part of the building is Elizabethan. The Godstone hotel is of a similar age and the Bell 18th century although there are some older parts around the back.

Sandstone, sand and fullers earth have been quarried in this locality as far back as Roman and Norman times. Our path goes by Bay Pond, a nature reserve owned by the Surrey Wildlife Trust. If you are lucky you may spot a heron fishing or resting on one of the islets. Beyond, you go past the church where there was a Saxon settlement. Down the hill you pass some more water and then John Evelyn's old Jacobean house at Leigh Place. The house is privately-owned and is not open to visitors. However, the black swans, ducks and geese are well-worth seeing from the public footpath. Soon after you can peep through a hedge on the right to see an old water mill and a short distance further on we circle an ancient earthwork. The mound is hidden in a sweet chestnut wood.

Later the footpath cuts through Godstone Farm where there is a wide selection of farmyard animals including pigs, sheep, goats and rabbits. You may wish to keep to the public path, or alternatively this is a good place to stop, for the farm has been primarily set up to interest and attract children. There is a charge for children but one adult can enter free if accompanied by a child. There is also an adventure play area. Whilst the children are being entertained the driver could walk on and collect the car.

Refreshments

There are the three inns mentioned above, in particular the Bell has a room and a good garden for children. Visitors to Godstone Farm can also obtain refreshments.

Route 15

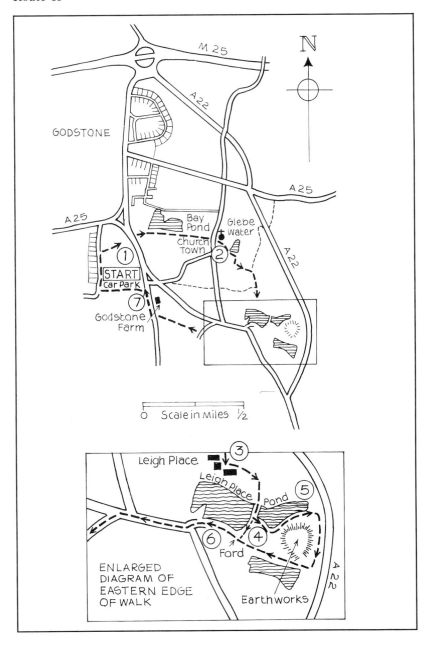

Route 15

Godstone and Leigh Place Pond

2¾ miles
(Variation 2¼ miles)

Start

At the Godstone car park south of the pond on the village green (GR 351515). The entrance is opposite the White Hart on the B2236 just south of the A25.

Route

1. *Cross the main road to the White Hart and follow the footpath marked to the Parish Church by the side of Godstone Village Hall. Bay Pond is on the left of the path before reaching the church.*

2. *Go by the right-hand side of the church. At the foot of the church yard, there is a yellow waymark which leads to the right of Glebe Water. Here you cross a humped-back bridge with white wrought iron fencing. The path turns right just before the locked gate on the left. The ground here can be muddy in wet weather. About 50 yards further on, take the left-hand fork. At the top of the field the path bears right through a wooded glade, then keeps along a well-marked path down the side of the field. There is another waymark in this field.*

3. *At the end of the path turn left on to the narrow metalled road. This road goes past John Evelyn's house, Leigh Place. Skirt the single storey brick building and at the end of the wire fence, turn right following the yellow waymarked path round the edge of the estate.*

4. *Soon this public footpath goes between the fenced estate and Leigh Place Pond. At the end of the pond turn left over the stile. (There is also a path straight on which cuts off about ½ mile from the walk.) About 45 yards on, if you look through the hedged fence, you can see a waterwheel to the right of the building. Turn left along the track. In the autumn look out for the many different fungi, including stinkhorns. Keep straight on where a track marked 'Private' turns left. The small hill above on the right is an ancient earthwork. The path going uphill below this fortification can be muddy in wet weather.*

5. *At the top of the hill is the Godstone-by-pass (A22). Turn right along the footpath and 15 yards further on turn right again through a kissing gate. The path is cleared from time to time but if overgrown with blackberries follow the embankment above the main road and turn right before the dip. The path then follows the Greensand Way downhill with the Castle Mound on the right. Follow the path with a pond on the left. Ignore the public bridleway on the right and paddle across the ford or use the footbridge. (The shorter walk joins just before this stream). The path emerges on to a metalled road which crosses the old millrace.*

6. *At the top of the hill turn right on the main road. Cross over the minor road to the right which points to Godstone Church but soon after, cross the major road just before a bridge and turn left. After the second house on the left take the marked footpath on the right. Climb up the hill through the wood. The path then goes straight across Godstone Farm. (If visiting you will need to pay. See page 00 for details).*

7. *At the main road turn right. At the bottom of the hill, turn left and follow the path by the stream until this emerges on a metalled road. Turn right and Godstone Green will soon be in sight.*

Public Transport
There are buses from Croydon to Godstone and some run on to East Grinstead. Also, there is a service Reigate, Godstone, Westerham.

Almshouses designed by Sir Gilbert Scott in Churchtown, Godstone

Farthing Down and Chaldon

Outline

Farthing Down − Chaldon Church − Tollsworth Manor − Fryern Farm −
Happy Valley − Farthing Down.

Summary

An interesting walk in an oasis of pretty countryside surrounded by trunk roads and
urban developments, with not too much hill climbing.

Attractions

We just go over the Surrey border on this walk. Farthing Down, an open space
provided by the City of London, was in the county of Surrey but is now in the London
Borough of Croydon. The car park is at the top of the ridge and is a good place for
kite flying. This grass top and the Happy Valley below are also good spots for playing
games in general. Further on we go through woodland and across open farmland. This
stretch can be muddy after the fields have been ploughed but it is well-worth
continuing into Surrey and Chaldon Church.

You must take your muddy boots off to visit the church. Founded in Saxon times,
St Peter and St Paul must be one of the most interesting churches of the early English
period. The picture on the west wall is famous as the earliest known English wall
painting. It dates from 1200 and is without equal in any other part of Europe. Children
should perhaps study this picture to see what their christian ancestors were brought
up to believe. It may even be salutory to reflect on the seven deadly sins and be on
good behaviour themselves.

Sadly the old bell, reputed to be the oldest in Surrey and over 750 years old, was
stolen in 1970. However there remains the old oak pulpit dated 1657 provided by
Patience Lambert of the Manor House. This is one of the very few specimens of
pulpits of Cromwelian times.

We then make our way across open farmland and a small wood before passing the
old manor house. Tollsworth Manor is privately occupied but it is still of interest from
the outside. Soon after we join the North Downs Way and look down on the cloverleaf
junction of the M23 and M25 before returning to the Happy Valley and our starting
point.

Refreshments

The Welcome Tea Rooms by the car park have been forced to close by the banks.
Eventually it is hoped something will arise from the ashes of this business.

Route 16

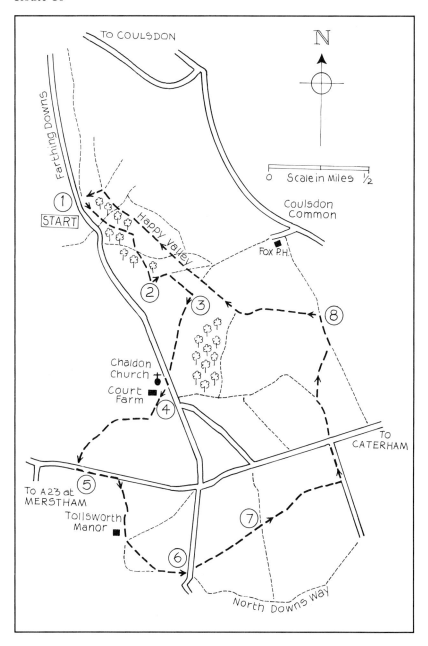

Route 16

Farthing Down and Chaldon

**6 miles
(Variation 2 miles)**

Start

The best approach for this walk is to go east off the A23 at Coulsdon on to the B276 *(Marlpit Lane)* and take the second turning right after going under the railway bridge. The unfenced road with cattle grids goes off to the left uphill almost immediately. The car park *(closed at dusk)* is on the right at the end of open downland *(GR 302572)*.

Route

1. From the car park cross the road and go downhill past the tea rooms. On reaching the first track turn right (signposted Happy Valley) and as you go through the Devilsden Wood ignore the path to the right with steps. However, take the second path, which only bears slightly to the right, and go straight on at the next crossroads of paths.

2. After crossing the two fields turn left downhill just inside the edge of the wood, with a field on the right-hand side. This path leads down to the Happy Valley but on reaching the open grassland turn right and go alongside the edge of the wood until your reach the next path.

3. Here you turn right. The signpost points to Chaldon Church. After going through a narrow stretch of woodland and two fields you will see the church in front of you.

4. By the small pond opposite the church there is a signpost to Alderstead Heath. Follow this path to the corner of the first field, then go along the right-hand fence of the second field. About 30 yards from the end of this field cut the corner off to a stile and make across this third field to a stile into a wood. Just inside the wood there is a junction of paths. Take the left hand one and make for the road.

5. Cross over the road and turn left, taking care with the oncoming traffic. At the first bridleway turn right off the road and just past Tollsworth Manor turn left. At the top of the field, after rounding a hedge, turn left on the North Downs Way. Below you will see the motorway complex.

6. At the next road, Hilltop Lane, you leave the long distance path. Turn left, and 50 yards on turn right by the side of Pilgrim's Lodge. Go over two stiles and then cross three fields diagonally to the left.

7. After leaving the last field by a stile you will see a footpath signpost marked five ways. Take the path marked to Caterham. On reaching a road turn left and at the

73

Troublesome sheep

end of this T-junction turn right on to a busier one. Almost immediately cross over to the footpath opposite. About 50 yards ahead look out for a gap in the hedge on the right-hand side and turn right on a well marked path making for the left-hand edge of some hospital buildings with a clump of conifers up the hillside on the other side of this path.

8. *At the top turn left and thirty yards further on, by some barracks, turn left again. At the bottom of the hill turn right into Happy Valley.*

9. *At the next junction a path crosses from the Fox public house to our original path to Chaldon Church. However, continue along the valley floor and near the end of Devilsden Wood, on the left, there is a signpost marked Farthing Down 300 yards. There is a steep grassy slope back to the car park but you can do a more gentle climb by following the contours.*

Variation

You can make a short walk of it by going as far as 3 and continuing down the hill and turning left at 9 back to the car.

Public Transport

There is no public transport over Farthing Down but there is a regular bus from Croydon to Godstone Green via Old Coulsdon where you could reach the walk from Coulsdon Common. Taking Fox Lane opposite you pass the Fox public house drop down to Happy Valley at 9 and if you go up the hill the other side you join the walk at 3. Coming back you could continue along the path by the barracks at 8 but it is more interesting to return to the Happy Valley before going home.

Useful information

Routes in order of difficulty

To the experienced walker only a few short walks in Surrey would be at all strenuous. Except for route 5 which has some steep hills on the longer walks and route 1 if you climb the Devil's Jumps, there is little to cause any problems. Six- and seven-year olds can try out some of the shorter walks before tackling the others. Route 2 is a figure of eight walk and could be done as two shorter ones if you fancied returning to the area. To help you choose the mileage for your walk these are listed in route order.

Route	Main Walk	Variation	Short
1	5	4	1½
2	7¼	4½	2¾
3	6	3	
4	7	5	
5	4	3½	2¼
6	5½		
7	6		2½
8	4½		2
9	3½		1¾
10	4		
11	4		2
12	5	4¼	
13	6½	3½	
14	6	5¼	1¾
15	2¾		2¼
16	6		2

The cricket green, Chiddingfold (walk 4)

Public Transport

Wherever possible I have tried to show you where you can join a walk with the aid of buses and trains. Some stations are closed on Sundays. Chilworth is closed. The other two on routes 4 and 11 were open at the time of writing but this may change if more savings have to be made. Similarly with buses; the Sunday service is very restricted or does not run at all. I have not mentioned the route numbers for these may change. Under the 1985 Transport Act bus operators are only required to give 42 days notice to introduce, alter or cancel services or individual journeys. Whilst the County Council is in existence it publishes helpful area travel booklets which are usually updated twice a year. Before planning a walk it is advisable to obtain an up-to-date timetable. These are available from bus enquiry offices, local libraries and borough district council offices throughout the country. The Travel Guides may also be obtained by post from the Passenger Transport Group, Highways Transportation Department, Surrey County Council, County Hall, Kingston upon Thames KT1 2DY. The booklet areas required for the various walks are: Waverley for routes 1 and 4; Guildford for routes 5 and 6; Mole Valley for routes 8 to 10; Tandridge, Reigate and Banstead for routes 11 to 16.

Wet weather alternatives

London is within easy travelling distance where there is such a vast range of attractions that there is an endless choice for any holiday break. Below are listed some local alternatives. Many are under cover but for some you would need fair weather.

Museums and other attractions

Alton over the county border has the Mid-Hants Steam Railway. This runs through ten miles of beautiful Hampshire countryside between Alton and Alresford. A variety of steam locomotives being restored may be seen at Ropley. Tel. 0962 734200.
Birdworld and Underwater World at Holt Pound south of Farnham. 17 acres of beautiful gardens and parkland housing a wide variety of birds and fish. Tel. 0420 22140.
Chatley Heath Semaphore Tower, Cobham was built in 1822 as one of a chain of towers for sending signals from the Admiralty in London to Portsmouth and Plymouth. Restored in 1989, it is open from noon as a museum in summer on Wednesdays, Saturdays, Sundays, Bank Holidays and Tuesdays following bank holidays. Tel. 0932 62762.
Cobham a recently-restored water mill on the River Mole east of the shopping area on the A245.
Farnham One of Surrey's most interesting and historic towns including the castle, formerly the seat of the Bishop of Winchester. Tel. castle 0252 721194 and castle keep 0252 713392.
Museum of Farnham in a magnificent Georgian town house, West Street. Displays of local history and archaeology, costumes and fine art. Tel. 0252 715094.
Godalming Museum, High Street, local history and archaeology. Tel. 0483 426510.
Guildford Behind the High Street lies a beautiful public garden with a castle. In medieval times this was a royal residence but now only a sixty foot high keep remains. A fine view over the town can be obtained from the top. Just below this lies the museum at Castle Arch, Quarry Street which has some coin in the slot working models and houses some local history and archaeology exhibits. Tel. 0483 444750.
Haslemere Museum, High Street, has collections of British birds, botany, zoology and geology. Excellent for children. Pond dipping for water creatures. Tel. 0428 642112.

Haxted Water Mill, Haxted, Lingfield. About two miles west of Edenbridge on the River Eden, 16th century water mill with working machinery and displays. June to September daily 12−5, weekends and bank holiday only during April and May.

Loseley House and Park, Elizabethan Mansion built of stone from Waverley Abbey also has a restaurant in a 17th century Tithe Barn, farm shop and tours. Tel. 0483 304440.

Outwood Post Mill − see walk 14.

Reigate Castle and the Barons Caves. All that remains is a mound with a dry moat in an attractive garden. The existing gateway was erected in 1777 using original stones from the site. Beneath the site caves were probably excavated for storage although parts may have been used as dungeons. The council have leased these to the Wealdon Cave and Mine Society. Details of opening times and entrance fees are obtainable in writing from the society c/o Mr M. Clark, 14 Smoke Lane, Reigate RH2 7HS.

Reigate Priory, Bell Street Originally built in 1235, was rebuilt in 1779 and is now a school with a small but popular museum. Only open during term time Wednesdays 2−4.30. Tel. 07372 45065.

Reigate Heath Windmill − see walk 13.

Tilford, Old Kiln Agriculture Museum, Reed Road, 10-acre site displaying village and rural life with arboretum, woodland walks and picnic areas. Open April to September Wednesdays, Sundays and Bank Holidays 11−6.

Wisley Royal Horticultural Society Garden is well-worth a visit any time of the year, 240 acres with a wide variety of gardens and greenhouses. Open all year except Christmas Day − members only Sundays. Tel. 0483 224234.

Steps to Leith Hill (walk 7)

77

National Trust Houses

The National Trust owns a number of properties in Surrey and a large area of picturesque land. A number of these walks touch or pass over their land. No doubt many of you enjoy using their facilities and it is hoped many will support the organisation. The following houses not far off the Guildford – Leatherhead road are well worth a visit.

Clandon Park, West Clandon, built in the Palladian style has been little altered since it was erected in the early 18th century.

Hatchlands, East Clandon, a mid-18th century house, the earliest known work of Robert Adam. Look carefully at the outside. One of the three sets of windows on the south side are dummies. You will notice that there are only two floors inside.

Polsden Lacey South of Great Bookham has 140 acres and a magnificent Regency house built in 1824 on the site of a house once owned by the 18th century playwright and actor Richard Brinsley Sheriden.

Hambledon Church (route 4)

78

Indoor Swimming with, at some centres, other sporting activities.

Banstead Sports Club, Merlin Rise Banstead. Tel. 07373 60950/59959.
Cranleigh Recreation Centre, Village Way, High Street. Tel. 0483 274400.
Dorking Swimming Centre, Reigate Road. Tel. 0306 887722.
Farnham Sports Centre, Dogflud Way, East Street. Tel. 0252 723208.
Godalming Leisure Centre, Summer Road, Farncombe in Broadwater Park next to the lake. Besides the indoor swimming pool there is an outdoor paddling pool and picnic area. Tel. 04868 7282.
Haslemere Sports Centre. Tel. 0428 642124.
Leatherhead Leisure Centre and Water Park, Guildford Road. In addition to indoor activities various types of boats can be hired on the large lake and on the smaller lake children's paddle boats and peanut rowing boats. Picnic area with paddling pool. Tel. 0372 377674.
Redhill Donyngs Recreation Centre, Linkfield Lane. Tel. 0737 764732.

Boating on River Wey

Various types of boats can be used for trips or hired from the following places. Key: narrow boat (N), launch (L), punt (P), dinghies (D), rowing boat (R), and canoe (C).
Farncombe Boat House, Catteshall Lock, Godalming, N, P, R, C. Tel. 04868 21306.
Godalming Packet Boat Company, Old Warehouse, Godalming Wharf, N. horsedrawn summer afternoon weekend 2 hour cruises — more in high summer. Tel. 04868 29098/25397.
Guildford Boat House, Millbrook — South of the Yvonne Arnaud Theatre. Trips L and N. Hire D, R, C. and N for holidays. Tel. 0483 504494.

River Thames

You can hire boats of all kinds at various places on the river. Several boathouses offer spring and summer river cruises. It is advisable to check on up to date timetables. The principal ones are:
French Brothers, The Runnymede Boathouse, Windsor Road, Old Windsor. Tel. 0753 851900. Runnymede to Hampton Court stopping at various places on the way and Runnymede to Windsor.
J.G.F. Passenger Boats, Cowey Sale, Walton on Thames. Tel. 081 543 0607. 45 minute summer scenic trips from Walton Bridge.
Salter River Steamers. Tel. 0753 865832. Leaves late morning from Victoria Gardens, Staines for Runnymede and Windsor returning in the afternoon. On the way the boat calls at Chertsey Bridge Lock and Egham Bell Weir Lock.
Turk Launches, Thames Side, Kingston upon Thames. Tel. 081 546 2434 run services between Hampton Court and Richmond.

THE FAMILY WALKS SERIES

The publishers welcome suggestions for further titles in this series; and will be pleased to consider manuscripts relating to Derbyshire from new or established authors.

Scarthin Books of Cromford, in the Peak District, are also leading second-hand and antiquarian booksellers, and are eager to purchase specialised material, both ancient and modern.

Contact Dr D.J. Mitchell, 0629-823272.